India, Pakistan, and the United States

India, Pakistan, and the United States

Breaking with the Past

Shirin R. Tahir-Kheli

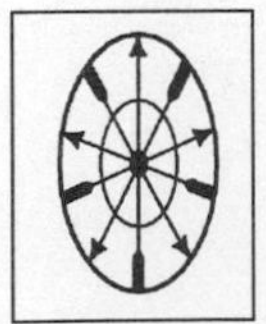

COUNCIL ON FOREIGN RELATIONS PRESS

NEW YORK

GN RELATIONS BOOKS

, is a nonprofit and nonpartisan organiza-
d understanding of international affairs through the free and civil exchange of ideas.

THE COUNCIL TAKES NO INSTITUTIONAL POSITION ON POLICY ISSUES AND HAS NO AFFILIATION WITH THE U.S. GOVERNMENT. ALL STATEMENTS OF FACT AND EXPRESSIONS OF OPINION CONTAINED IN COUNCIL BOOKS ARE THE SOLE RESPONSIBILITY OF THE AUTHORS OR SIGNATORIES.

From time to time books, monographs, and reports written by members of the Council's research staff or others are published as a "Council on Foreign Relations Book." Any work bearing that designation is, in the judgment of the Committee on Studies of the Council's Board of Directors, a responsible treatment of a significant international topic.

For further information on Council publications, please write the Council on Foreign Relations, 58 East 68th Street, New York, NY 10021, or call the Publications Office at (212) 434-9400.

Printed in the United States of America.

Library of Congress Cataloging-in-Publication Data

Tahir-Kheli, Shirin R.

India, Pakistan, and the United States: Breaking with the Past/Shirin R. Tahir-Kheli.

p. cm.

ISBN 0-87609-199-0

1. United States—Foreign relations—India. 2. India—Foreign relations—United States. 3. United States—Foreign relations—Pakistan. 4. Pakistan—Foreign relations—United States. 5. United States—Foreign relations—1945–1989. 6. United States—Foreign relations—1989– 7. Cold War. I. Council on Foreign Relations. II. Title.

E183.8.I4S455 1997

327.73054—dc21 97-3927

CIP

---

96 97 98 99 PB 10 9 8 7 6 5 4 3 2 1

In memory of my mother, Khurshid Raziuddin Siddiqi, who remained my best friend

Contents

Foreword

RECOGNIZING ITS NEED TO PAY INCREASED ATTENTION to developments in South Asia, the Council on Foreign Relations organized a study group in 1993 that met periodically over the following year. The deliberations of that group, which assembled a number of South Asian experts, revealed that even among experts, some of the intricacies of Pakistani-Indian bilateral relations were not well understood. We also discovered that the interrelations of American, Indian, and Pakistani foreign policies had been slighted in the literature.

America's bilateral relations with Pakistan and with India have been analyzed by several writers. This is the first book, we believe, that has systematically attempted to trace the interplay between Washington, New Delhi, and Islamabad as their often tumultuous relations have played out.

This text tracks certain of the major issues of South Asia over the past generation: nuclear weapons developments, Afghanistan, and Kashmir. It pays special attention to the new energies that New Delhi and Islamabad have invested in economic reform, a development that offers some promise in building a sounder bilateral relationship between these two major powers of the subcontinent.

At the moment when the second Clinton administration in Washington is reviewing its options and priorities in foreign affairs, the Council believes that Shirin Tahir-Kheli's account will be helpful to it and the general public.

Richard W. Murphy
Hasib J. Sabbagh Senior Fellow for the Middle East
Council on Foreign Relations

Preface

WHILE INDIA AND PAKISTAN ATTRACT LESS INTERnational attention than they did during the Cold War, American interests in these two states remain highly significant. They both have nuclear weapons capability, and they are in a volatile area of the world, adjacent to the Persian Gulf and China. Both New Delhi and Islamabad hold commercial importance and economic potential for the West. Normalization between India and Pakistan thus would greatly contribute to stability in the region and benefit the international community.

This book analyzes the triangular relationship among the United States, India, and Pakistan. It examines the American record of helping improve the Indo-Pak relationship despite their strained relations throughout a half century of cold peace and intermittent war. For nearly 40 years the United States and the Soviet Union competed for influence in South Asia; in the 1960s and 1970s, the superpowers pursued policies that did little to diminish the antagonism between Indians and Pakistanis. In 1954, the United States signed a defense pact that gave Pakistan membership in the Central Treaty Organization (CENTO) and the

South East Asia Treaty Organization (SEATO). This gave Pakistan a measure of protection against Soviet threats and, in the process, annoyed India. China played an important role in the region as Pakistan's friend and supporter, as a counter to Soviet influence, and, after the 1962 border conflict between China and India, as a challenge to India. In 1971, India signed a Treaty of Friendship with the Soviet Union that proved useful during that year's Indo-Pak war and in the subsequent creation of Bangladesh.

In the 1980s, the clash of American and Soviet interests erupted in Afghanistan. The Reagan administration viewed the 1979 Soviet invasion as a deliberate attempt by the Soviet Union to extend its empire into the Gulf region and worked, at considerable cost, to expel the Red Army from its powerful position in the area. For nearly a decade, the principal objective of American policy in the subcontinent was to force Soviet withdrawal, enlisting China, Egypt, and Saudi Arabia in support of that goal. Despite heavy U.S. support for Pakistan as an ally in the anti-Soviet campaign, the 1980s also saw a major American attempt to enhance the U.S. relationship with India. Washington proved surprisingly able to improve relations with India and Pakistan simultaneously; through the use of its good offices, it facilitated a modest rapprochement between the two.

The onset of the uprising in Kashmir in 1989, however, wiped out friendly feelings between India and Pakistan. India's unwillingness to acknowledge the anger of many Muslim Kashmiris at their treatment by Delhi, in tandem with Pakistan's readiness to exploit and further the insurgency, brought the two to the brink of confrontation. Washington was unwilling to insert itself into the squabbles of the subcontinent but was determined to halt the spread of nuclear weapons. As the verbal battles between India and Pakistan were raging, the United States cut off its assistance to Pakistan because of the latter's nuclear program.

The end of the Cold War brought new opportunities for reconciliation between India and Pakistan and has underlined the fact that the United States remains essential to future peace in the subcontinent. There are no alternatives. Russia is friendly to India but is viewed with suspicion in Pakistan. China has good credentials in

Pakistan and has been trying since 1987 to make headway in its relations with India. However, the continued border problem between China and India and China's reported help to Pakistan in sensitive areas—from Afghanistan to defense—continue to make many in India wary of Beijing's intentions. Iran has carefully cultivated good relations with both of the largest states in the subcontinent, yet the Islamic fervor contained in Iran's message makes both Islamabad and New Delhi somewhat uncomfortable. Japan has an economic role in the future of South Asia and is therefore interested in developing peaceful ties among all South Asian states. However, Japan has been careful to limit its position to one of economic diplomacy.

To engage in a peace process involving India and Pakistan, the United States must break with its practice of concentrating on South Asian issues only in periods of high tension such as those caused by regional wars, Soviet occupation, or the threat of nuclear-related crises. Regionally, the inhibitions on bold thinking in both capitals and the freewheeling intelligence agencies of both have complicated the task of reconciliation. Nonetheless, the new generation of Pakistanis and Indians is aware of the opportunity to break from the past and work for a better future. They want to encourage foreign investment and economic development. They hope that their respective economic programs will help unfreeze traditional positions on the politically intractable problem of Kashmir and their respective nuclear weapons programs. These South Asians understand that peace is an essential requirement for economic progress and that potential conflict between India and Pakistan makes investors hesitant.

Making the case for Washington's sustained involvement will indeed be difficult unless both states make a concerted attempt to engage one another. Yet it is also evident that the American national interest will be best served by a policy aimed at diminishing these historic tensions. Success would yield important dividends in dealing with the nuclear issues and in providing a large market for U.S. goods and services. Furthermore, in the absence of the superpower competition that bid up the costs of past American involvement in the subcontinent, the opportunity now exists to make greater headway with less outlay. With patience and commitment, the United States should be able to cut through the problems in Indo-Pakistan relations.

A study group dealing with these issues in the relations among Pakistan, India, and the United States met at the Council on Foreign Relations between September 1993 and June 1994 and was co-chaired by Senior Fellow Richard Murphy and me. I am particularly grateful to the following participants for their insights: Ambassador William Clark, Gobind Nankani, Shahid Javed Burki, Toufiq Siddiqi, Paula Newberg, Mitchell Reiss, and Prem Shankar Jha. The book is not a synthesis of their views but reflects their awareness that there is a gap in American understanding of relations between the two most populous states in South Asia and that greater knowledge must precede a constituency for sustained interest in Washington.

This is not a study of bilateral U.S. relations with India or Pakistan. Our focus, as stated, is on the triangular relationship rather than the policies of all states with important stakes in India and Pakistan. I have offered an analysis of the U.S.-India-Pakistan triad because I believe that it will determine the future direction for South Asia. The years from 1980 to 1992 are examined in some detail because it was in this 12-year period that this rare, three-way interaction was most vigorous. Consequently, this is where it is most useful to lay out the India and Pakistan cases side by side.

In the various chapters, there exists an asymmetry in American prominence. The United States looms large in the economic chapter, for example, while at other times, such as in the discussion of political factors, there is relatively little mention of the American connection. The explanation is simple. India and Pakistan designed their economic reforms with the United States very much in mind, opening up their economies in the 1990s against the background of communism's collapse. They specifically targeted American investment and the response has justified their expectations. However, when the political map of India and of Pakistan was forged in the early years after independence in 1947, America was largely absent from the scene and these states developed along certain paths based on local preferences and history.

Among the Council staff, I want to thank Ashok Chaudhari and Shugu Imam for all of their early help with our work. Audrey

McInerny and Elmira Bayrasli served ably as rapporteurs, and Nomi Colton-Max helped with fine-tuning and editing the manuscript and seeing this project through to completion. Special thanks are owed to the Center of International Studies at Princeton University and to its director, John Waterbury, for the facilities and the intellectual climate that few other fellowships provide. The Foreign Policy Research Institute has provided support and understanding, and its president, Harvey Sicherman, has been a tutor and a friend in matters relating to the Middle East and South Asia for decades, both in and out of our respective periods in the U.S. government. Leo Rose, Robert Oakley, and Phillips Talbot read the manuscript and offered valuable suggestions. Steve Aoki's comments on the nuclear chapter served to refine the work. V.S. Arunachalam, Keshab Mahindra, Raja Mohan, Mani Shankar Aiyar, and many other officials and colleagues were generous with their time and friendship throughout my many visits to India. Various officials, colleagues, and friends in Pakistan have helped increase my understanding of events and issues. In particular, I want to thank General Mahmud Ali Durrani for his insights regarding the manuscript's handling of the Zia period. I am grateful to all these scholars and policymakers for their help.

Finally, this is not a shorthand primer for the U.S. government in the immediate management of relations with India and Pakistan, although it is my aim to increase understanding of the dynamic that governs our relations with South Asia and offer options for future policy. I hope to provide those long interested in the subcontinent, and others who may be engaging their attention on South Asia essentially for the first time, with some of the key issues and a touch of the rich detail that is woven into the fabric of relations among the United States, India, and Pakistan.

Shirin Tahir-Kheli
January 1997

Introduction

WHAT IS THE STAKE FOR THE UNITED STATES IN INDIA and Pakistan, and how has the end of the Cold War influenced American foreign policy? Because perceptions of policy and opportunity differ, depending on whether the prism of viewing is New Delhi, Islamabad, or Washington, it is important to assess each of these in turn.

Indian foreign policy in the early years after independence in 1947 was shaped by the just-beginning Cold War. Having achieved the end of colonial rule, Indian leaders felt a special sense of mission in the subcontinent and in the Third World beyond. While India sought a cooperative future relationship with its former colonial power, Britain, the focus of Indian policy was elsewhere. There were early signs that India would have liked a good relationship with the United States. Indian leaders were aware that the United States had exerted pressure on Britain to advance the date of withdrawal from the subcontinent. But the chance to build a solid bridge to Washington faded because of the American concerns about communism and Soviet and (after 1949) Chinese expansionist designs, concerns that New Delhi did not necessarily share.

The very nature of the Indian independence movement ensured that Indian leaders would have a natural affinity for the continuing struggle of other aspiring movements in Asia, Africa, and Latin America. India saw itself as a model for other emerging countries, and its first prime minister, Jawaharlal Nehru, was one of the founding members of the Non-Aligned Movement (NAM), which sought to navigate the shoals of the Cold War. Consequently Washington quickly became suspicious of Indian policy. In the Dulles era, the United States was unwilling to accept that there could be a middle way. For Washington, the choice was simple: the free world, led by the United States, or the Communist world, led by the Soviet Union. After the Communist victory in China in 1949, the United States was concerned with the importance of the People's Republic of China to the NAM and the special links that movement bestowed on Sino-Indian relations. In addition, American concerns were exacerbated by the Korean War and the growing Soviet nuclear capability, thereby setting the stage for an urgent American search for allies, which brought Pakistan into Washington's focus.

Throughout the 1950s and early 1960s, when nonalignment was a major force in international relations, India was often its articulate spokesman and effectively campaigned on behalf of Third World countries for its policies. India was active in international institutions, where it sought to build bridges between the developed and the developing world. Its effectiveness as a conciliator in the East-West competition was circumscribed by the unwillingness of American leaders to respect nonalignment as a viable policy and U.S. annoyance with India's "lecturing" to it.

The Third World was a key arena for East-West competition. As the Cold War continued, India was increasingly cast as an American adversary. In India's eyes, the U.S. search for allies led it to choose Pakistan in the subcontinent. India's unhappiness with that choice stemmed from New Delhi's conviction that the supply of American arms and other military assistance would bear directly on the relationship between India and Pakistan. Indian leaders criticized the American tendency, as they saw it, to align itself with the nondemocratic regimes around the world, including those in Pakistan. It puzzled many that Washington and New Delhi, the world's two largest democracies, could not cooperate better in the political arena. The United States did try to compensate for the thrust of its support for Pakistan by becoming a major supporter of Indian economic development plans, granting it more than $10 billion in assistance. Despite such attempts and the American willingness to write off a large portion of the ensuing debt, the political relationship between New Delhi and Washington failed to evolve positively and the United States chafed at Indian criticism while believing there was no similar criticism of the Soviet Union.[1] For example, when the Soviets invaded Hungary in 1956, India was much less perturbed than it was when the United States moved to further American interests in other parts of the world, such as Vietnam. Similarly, when the Soviets invaded Afghanistan in 1979, India failed to join in the near-universal condemnation. Afghanistan brought Pakistan and the United States into even closer alliance as it transformed Pakistan in to a "front-line" state.

Jawaharlal Nehru was a world-class leader whose fascination with the socialist model for development increasingly led him to seek Soviet assistance in the public sector. He found the Soviet Union more than willing to support India's special needs in trade and aid while Washington offered assistance to Pakistan.

China was another important player on the South Asian scene. It pursued friendship with India and then collaborated in developing the "spirit of Bandung," named for the Indonesian venue of the first NAM meeting, in 1955. China expected that India, having given up its special relationship with Tibet, would accept all Chinese actions there. However, in 1959, a crackdown in Tibet led to the Dalai Lama's flight to India, where Nehru allowed him to stay. Despite the expansion of Sino-Indian relations throughout the 1950s, the states became competitive over time. Finally, an open clash in October 1962 caught the Indians off guard. Chinese gains in the 1962 border war and the trauma of what many Indians regard as Chinese treachery made it nearly impossible to forget the humiliation. That plus the October 1964 nuclear test by China strengthened the lobby in India for the development of nuclear weapons. The testing of the Indian "peaceful" nuclear device in 1974 made India a major regional nuclear player and sufficiently threatened Pakistan, but it failed to satisfy those Indians who argued for further development in the face of the full-fledged Chinese nuclear capability. These nuclear hawks argued that China had to be dealt with, especially as later allegations surfaced of China's willingness to help in Pakistan's nuclear program.[2]

In the first three decades after independence, India was ably led at the national level. Expectations of conflict with Pakistan necessitated a watchful eye on regional politics as both countries cultivated their respective cadres of friends and allies. Indians believed that a close relationship between the United States and Pakistan was against India's interest, and they also understood that Pakistan sought to exploit American concerns with the communist threat in order to build American support against any threat from India.

The Soviet invasion of Afghanistan and the vigorous response of the United States changed the rules of the game in the subcontinent. Beyond triggering a surge in U.S. support for Pakistan, the invasion shifted the focus of Soviet efforts there. Where earlier India had been the primary recipient of Soviet military and political support in South Asia, after 1979 Afghanistan became the main preoccupation. China, on the other hand, worried about containing the Soviet Union. This fear, compounded by its earlier border problems with India, led China to supply Pakistan with diplomatic and materiel support. The fact that Afghanistan was a small, nonaligned country made the Soviet action difficult to accept, and India became involved in the war. It provided the only non-Soviet air link to the Afghan capital, Kabul, and those Afghans who could afford to do so sought refuge in New Delhi from the violence at home. Furthermore, as the Indian government constantly reminded the United States, the upgrading of the Pakistani military machine had direct consequences for India. India viewed the provision of American F-16 fighter aircraft, for example, simply as a contribution to Pakistan's arsenal for any future war between India and Pakistan where airpower was likely to remain a crucial factor.

In the aftermath of the Soviet invasion, the Indian prime minister, Indira Gandhi, recognized that it was necessary to adjust Indian foreign policy. One early manifestation of her new approach was reflected in her 1982 meeting with the American president, Ronald Reagan, at Cancún, Mexico. Despite their very different political histories and personal philosophies, the meeting went extremely well. Whether it changed Indian perspectives immediately or not, it did leave Reagan pondering the intriguing possibilities of edging the United States closer to a declared friend of the Soviet Union and also helped mute the Indo-Pakistani conflict. Gandhi saw no real reason why a more robust relationship between the world's two largest democracies could not be fashioned. At the same time, she found Washington more willing to respect India's role as a regional leader (perhaps in part because the NAM had already lost its earlier cachet). New Delhi also reckoned that friendship with the United States would check the potential for excessive U.S. support of Pakistan. The political map of the region changed in 1979 with the fall of Iran's shah, a supporter of the United States. New Delhi did not want to see Pakistan's president, General Zia-ul Haq, replace him as a strong protector of American interest in the region. By the mid-1980s, India's need for a faster pace of technological development provided another important incentive for better relations with the United States.

Pakistan had focused its efforts to build a close relationship with the United States much earlier than had New Delhi. To compensate for its limited military capability and seeking a shield against a larger and more powerful neighbor, Islamabad reached for an outside protector. The Cold War offered the possibility, and successive leaders energetically cultivated an American-Pakistani alliance. This astute policy served Pakistan well as the state received economic and military support. Moreover, American support improved Pakistan's political posture as Pakistan became a member of the Baghdad Pact (1954–58) and of the South East Asia Treaty Organization (SEATO; 1955–71). In return, Pakistan's signature on a mutual defense agreement with Washington in 1959 gave the United States access to facilities to monitor the Soviet Union. These defense arrangements led to the Indian charge that Pakistan had introduced the Cold War into the subcontinent. Pakistan responded that it would be remiss if it did not seek all possible support for its own national interest. As it had done following the 1962 Sino-Indian war, Pakistan moved deliberately to cement its ties with China and proudly pointed to China's support in the 1965 war with India as indicative of the deep and abiding nature of the relationship.

As a Muslim country whose creation had been rooted in the demand for a separate homeland for the Muslims of India, Pakistan's strong relationship with other Islamic countries was expected. Yet while actively pursuing that goal, Pakistan was not notably successful. Many Muslim countries within the NAM were friends of India, and some—such as Egypt and Indonesia—were not pleased with Pakistan's cultivation of relations with Arab monarchies. Only after the oil price increase of 1973 and the new emphasis on Islamic unity did Islamabad's links with the oil-rich kingdoms and other Muslim states pay off. Pakistan proudly held the first Islamic summit in Lahore in 1973, with a broad agenda focusing on economic and political issues.

Pakistan's intricate pattern of foreign policy relationships in the 1970s, which included befriending Moscow, was shattered by the direct involvement of Soviet troops in Afghanistan in December 1979. At the time, no one foresaw that it would be the last major act of Soviet adventurism. There was an extensive negative international response, and Pakistan's role in fashioning the challenge to the occupation became central. Pakistani leaders, and President Zia in particular, believed the Soviet move into Afghanistan was merely the first stop in the Soviet march to the Indian Ocean. Zia kept a map of the Persian Gulf region in his study to show foreign visitors. It depicted a superimposed red cutout in the shape of Afghanistan. Unless the Soviets were seriously challenged, he asserted, the entire map would quickly go red. Zia believed this assertion; it was not simply a gimmick. Washington also shared his concern. The match between American goals and Pakistani objectives changed the relationship between the two nations. Rolling back the Soviet invasion thus became a key priority of the Reagan presidency; Reagan felt deeply that the "evil empire" must not enjoy the fruit of its aggression.

For the next decade, Pakistani policy makers cooperated intimately with the United States in Afghanistan. Their fear of a second front developing with India deepened Islamabad's sense of vulnerability. Objectively, there was little reason to assume Indian support for the Soviets, but Zia worried about the Indian-Soviet treaty of 1971. As insurance, he accelerated the Pakistani nuclear program, clearly conscious of the advantage that the

Indian nuclear test of 1974 had provided Delhi and despite the fact that he recognized that stepping over the nuclear threshold could provoke an Indian attack on his nuclear weapons facilities and also create severe complications in his relations with the United States.

Pakistan worked hard to multiply its options. It strengthened ties with China. It made a serious attempt to befriend some key countries in the Islamic world, such as Saudi Arabia and Egypt. The Organization of the Islamic Conference (OIC), headquartered in Jeddah, Saudi Arabia, became an important vehicle for pressure on the Soviet Union to withdraw from Afghanistan and raised the diplomatic price for the Soviets. Islamabad also benefited from the international exposure offered by the confrontation over the Soviet occupation of Afghanistan. It championed the rights of small, non-aligned countries as Pakistan made inroads into the NAM. Its success was evident in the successive annual votes at the General Assembly of the United Nations after 1980, which overwhelmingly (in the range of 116 in favor, 18 abstaining, and 8 against) called for Soviet withdrawal.

By the mid-1980s, pressure on the Soviets was beginning to tell. With outside assistance, the Afghan resistance fighters, the *Mujahidin*, were taking a toll on Soviet forces, and it was not clear that the latter could ever prevail. Soviet domestic politics began to favor withdrawal; the Gorbachev era began with an admission of failure in Afghanistan and questioned the wisdom of the occupation. The avenue of retreat for Moscow through the U.N.-sponsored "proximity talks" finally brought about the return of troops to the Soviet Union in 1989.[3]

Once direct Soviet presence was no longer an issue and the potential threat to American interests in the Persian Gulf had evaporated, the political importance of the region diminished for the United States. The very nature of the Soviet state was under challenge, and historic changes were in the making. President Reagan believed that the Soviet empire was falling apart as a result of the pressures the United States and its friends had brought to bear against the occupation of Afghanistan. In any event, the consequences went far beyond Afghanistan; they altered the East-West competition and changed the map of Europe.

The demise of the Soviet Union had a further immediate impact on the subcontinent. Traditionally the Soviet Union had been India's main supplier of major military equipment and spare parts; the Indian military was nearly 80 percent reliant on the Soviet Union. With its collapse, obtaining the requisite materiel became more difficult. India had been a willing buyer of Soviet oil and other resources and had to renegotiate a host of separate agreements with a variety of successor states instead of just one with a centralized Soviet regime. Moreover, India had long enjoyed favorable trade terms with the Soviet Union; now New Delhi feared that it could lose not only these terms but a large trading partner. While there had already been some moves to strengthen trade with the United States (by the mid-1980s, the United States had already become India's largest trading partner, with a volume of $5 billion annually in two-way trade), India's large public-sector enterprises missed the sizable Soviet market.

Narasimha Rao became the leader of the Congress Party after the assassination of Rajiv Gandhi and was elected prime minister after the 1991 election. Rao undertook bold economic reforms that had seemed unthinkable earlier and firmly set his country on a path of liberalization. The result was more than $2.5 billion in foreign investments in India with the promise of much more to come.

The collapse of the Soviet Union also affected Pakistan. On the positive side was the reduced fear of Soviet interference, which had obsessed Pakistan during the 1980s. On the negative side, Pakistan soon realized that the Americans would pay much less attention to the subcontinent in general and to it in particular. Pakistani leaders still feared trouble with India and were unable to find any new sources of support to make up for the loss of American interest. On top of that, there were very few ways left with which to reengage the United States after it cut off its assistance in 1990 because of Pakistan's nuclear program.

Several U.S. interests and objectives in South Asia did not change with the end of the Cold War. The United States remained interested in the growth of strong, stable, and independent states ready to live in peace with each other without outside interference. The 1962 Sino-India border war and the Indo-Pakistani wars of 1965 and 1971 left the United States concerned with the potential for future conflict in an area where the belligerents are states capable of producing nuclear weapons. Support for democracy and the development of sound political institutions continue to be American goals. Economic development and a higher standard of living for the people of this populous region remain important. American interests continue to be served by India remaining democratic and secular and by Pakistan remaining a moderate Islamic state and at the same time attempting to build democratic institutions. These regional goals are in consonance with broader U.S. objectives of nuclear nonproliferation, support for human rights and democracy, increased opportunities for American trade and investment, containment of radical religious movements, control and reduction of narcotics, and peaceful resolution of regional conflicts.

While the end of the Cold War clearly altered the importance of India and Pakistan to the United States, South Asia's size and population, its nuclear capability, and its geographic location as neighbor to the oil-rich Persian Gulf on the one side and the dynamic region to the east all ensure continuing U.S. concern.

1

Government and Politics

SOUTH ASIANS GENERALLY EXPECT AMERICAN POLICY to reflect an overriding interest in democracy throughout the world. Thus, they are often at a loss to understand why the United States finds it necessary to make an investment in nondemocratic regimes. The difference in the American approach to India and Pakistan illustrates the frequent dichotomy of the American policy—an emphasis on democracy but an appreciation of the need for close cooperation with authoritarian regimes when American interests so dictate. This chapter deals briefly with the subcontinent's political milieu, which provides the context for the foreign policy discussion that follows.

INDIA

Political development in India followed a track different from that of Pakistan, where the rules of the political game remain in transition and largely undefined. In India, the stature of the political elite that brought independence assured its supremacy within the democratic context. Despite the open nature of the political system, the

Congress Party, which spearheaded the independence movement, was repeatedly returned to power by the voters as the party of choice at the national level with only two exceptions in the first five decades (the 1977–79 stint of the Janata Party and the National Front government of the 1989–91 period). Within Congress, Jawaharlal Nehru and his heirs dominated the political scene. Only with the death of Rajiv Gandhi, Nehru's grandson, did power shift to Narasimha Rao, who had earlier served in the Gandhi cabinet. The Congress Party remained the dominant force until the 1996 elections, when a fractured verdict reflected a severe challenge from a variety of regional sources.

India's large size and diverse ethnic and religious mix strained the fabric of politics there, but the system was based on accommodating the tension under rules that favored the central government in New Delhi while granting considerable autonomy to the state governments.[1] Democracy provided the cement holding together the polyglot nation with a population of 880 million and more than 20 major languages.

The constitution of the republic, adopted in 1950, provides for a bicameral legislature. The 250-member upper house, the Rajya Sabha (the Council of States), is overshadowed by the more powerful lower house, the Lok Sabha (the People's Council), with 545 members. The latter plays the key role in the legislative process since finance bills can be introduced only there.

The Indian president is the head of state and is elected for a five-year term by a majority of members of the state legislative assemblies and of parliament. He can be reelected. He appoints and can dismiss the prime minister. Despite important functions, such as determining who forms the government when there is no clear mandate, the powers of the president are carefully circumscribed.

Under the parliamentary system, Indian prime ministers traditionally have wielded political power. Over the years, however, their authority has been reduced commensurately with their majority within parliament. Gone are the days when the Congress Party had a substantial majority and hence a freer hand.

In a country the size and complexity of India, challenges to the central government's authority are predictable at the state level. While such challenges were few in the first decades after independence, they have intensified in the last decade. Reassertion of state power often led New Delhi to dismiss state governments and impose "president's rule" there. Examples of the latter can be found in Bengal in 1967; in the Punjab in 1967, 1980, and 1987; in Assam in 1990; in Tamil Nadu in 1976 and 1990; and in Kashmir in 1986. As the March 1995 state elections indicated, the results brought into power political parties at variance with the larger centrist party, the Congress Party. The state elections were fought on the basis of regional and ethnic issues peculiar to each state. In addition, the manipulation of state politics by the Congress Party leadership at the center became an issue. With the end of charismatic leadership in the Congress Party, as exemplified by the Nehru family, it became difficult for the party's leader to impose personal control over the vast state party structure.

U.S. policy makers and scholars have wondered what makes it possible for India to deal with the stresses existing between an ancient civilization and a modern political system. Unlike what has happened in so many states that became independent in the 1950s and 1960s, Indian institutions have endured.

India was fortunate to have inherited a developed civilian bureaucracy from the British raj. Despite the vast migration of 1947, the system did not need to be re-created. Delhi was the established seat of government, and the civil service an elite institution well versed in the art of governance. The bureaucracy helped translate Delhi's writ over the vast and populous land. Initially, the civil servants were very much in the British mold. Their absorption of India and India's absorption of them took time.

The remnants of the British military infrastructure existed primarily in the Indian part of the subcontinent. Some units from the British Indian Army had seen action in the Far East in World War II. There were no solely Muslim divisions that could be neatly transferred to Pakistan, but the Indian army had Muslim companies and battalions. At independence, most Muslim officers as well as those in the noncommissioned and enlisted ranks were selected for dispatch to Pakistan. Muslim units stationed in what became Pakistan were inducted in their entirety into the Pakistan armed forces. The bulk of Muslims remained as part of the Indian military establishment where the officer corps, made up of Muslims, Hindus, and Sikhs, had trained together under the British.

Problems with Pakistan and a long border with China gave the Indian military an early sense of a national mission. However, even as its share of the defense budget rose, giving a disproportionate amount to the military establishment, there was civilian oversight of the military. The prime minister often retained the defense portfolio. Even when he did not—for example, under Nehru when Krishna Menon was the minister for defense—the service chiefs were subordinate to the civilian hierarchy. Political ambitions of the military were sharply curtailed as the political leadership provided continuity and respected leadership in the formative days of the Indian union.[2]

Although the Congress Party remained in power, other political parties on both the left and the right in the political spectrum were given a place in the democratic framework. The Communist Party of India (CPI) on the left and the old Jan Sangh on the right were two such examples. While these and other parties appealed to various segments of the Indian voting public, based on ethnic, caste, and communal lines, the Congress Party remained an umbrella institution with an appeal that lasted well into the 1970s, when the rise of linguistic and state-based parties began. Nehru's standing as the dynamic leader of modern India and the sense of a common destiny for all Indians kept the Congress Party in power even through the difficult period following the Sino-Indian border conflict in October 1962.

Nehru's successors did not possess his charisma. They also faced a more restive electorate. As independence receded from the minds of a new generation of Indians who took their system for granted, the margin for the Congress Party in elections was reduced. More parochial concerns replaced the national vision of the early decade. Indira Gandhi showed less support for democracy, promulgated a state of emergency in the mid-1970s, and put measures in place that were considered unacceptable.[3] The first Congress Party defeat in 1979 was the direct result of this state of emergency. The Janata government's two-year tenure did not break the Congress Party's hold on the system; however, it did demonstrate that India could survive without the Congress Party in power.

Indian institutions held together even as politics took a violent turn and religious fundamentalism surfaced. The system came under increasing attack from extremism, and the tradition of secularism in politics seemed to be its first casualty. In the Punjab, Mrs. Gandhi ordered the military to move against the Golden Temple, the holiest shrine of the Sikhs. Violence and polarization of the Sikhs continued, and in October 1984 Mrs. Gandhi herself fell victim, when she was assassinated by Sikh members of her security detail. In Kashmir, often described as a model of Indian secularism, elections were manipulated to ensure a Congress Party victory. Radicalization of politics followed the 1987 election in Kashmir, with the Jammu and Kashmir Liberation Front (JKLF) increasing its profile among the dissident youth who called for independence from India. Such alienation had a dramatic impact, given the history of Kashmir and its effect on Indo-Pakistan relations.

Hindu-Muslim relations were hurt by the rise of the extremist Hindu parties that preached the rhetoric of confrontation along communal lines rather than the rhetoric of conciliation of the early Congress Party years. Many of these right-wing parties built their newfound strength on anti-Muslim sentiments. One such Hindu organization, for example, the Vishwa Hindu Parishad (VHP), called in 1986 for the destruction of the centuries-old Babri mosque in Ayodhya and its replacement with a Hindu temple on the site declared to be the birthplace of Ram, the god-king hero. The government in Delhi allowed the VHP to lay the foundations of the temple in November 1989, even though the Ayodhya dispute was in the courts at the time. Mainstream parties, such as the Bharatiya Janata Party (BJP), joined in the call for the extremists to regain sacred ground in Ayodhya. With a weak central government unwilling to prevent the mosque's destruction, Ayodhya swiftly became the gravest test to date of India's secular policy. The issue ended the brief tenure of the National Front government of V.P. Singh. Although the Congress Party came back to power after the 1991 election, it was not under Rajiv Gandhi, who had fought the election for it. Following his assassination in May 1991 by Tamil extremists, Narasimha Rao won the election for the Congress Party.

The party found that communal divisions were difficult to bridge. A boisterous fundamentalism began to replace secularism.

Muslims, a minority of 120 million, often felt unprotected by the constitution, while Hindu extremists exploited memories of several centuries of Muslim rule. The Muslims held the Congress Party accountable for the destruction of the mosque at Ayodhya and the failure to protect secularism, which was the hallmark of earlier Congress Party stints in power. All over India there were large pockets of discontent. Insurgencies in the northeast challenged the writ of the government in New Delhi. In Kashmir, the insurgency challenged integration of that state within India; in the Punjab, the wounds from the Golden Temple assault were still bleeding; India's direct involvement against dissident Tamils in neighboring Sri Lanka had left a seething dislike among India's Tamils for the Congress Party, under whose tenure the action took place. Elections in November 1993 and March 1995 at the state level demonstrated how far the party's fortunes had fallen as it lost several key states. For many, the results demonstrated popular discontent over the slow progress in dealing with the issues of poverty and unemployment. For others, the results were a harbinger of the high domestic costs of the reform process, much lauded outside India. Nevertheless, cohesion in the continuation of the system was demonstrated, even in the face of deep alienation, such as in Kashmir. All in all, Indian democracy has prevented the breakup of the state even as it has allowed challenges to traditional authority. Throughout the rough and tumble of the Congress Party's control, its power base continued to erode.

The collapse of the Congress government of Narasimha Rao in the 1996 election was also a mandate against the increase of central authority at the expense of state leadership and regional issues. A variety of explanations have been advanced for the debacle, from scandals involving key national political leaders (meaning the electorate's general disillusionment with political leaders of both major parties, particularly with those from the Congress Party), to the local leadership in the various states finally feeling strong enough to stand up to New Delhi. Other explanations offer the reaction against "federal fundamentalists" who, over the years, believed that states were merely an extension of central authority. The end of charismatic leadership meant that regional and local differences could not be bridged and a national mandate for the party in power could not be created.

The 1996 election gave the Congress Party 136 seats, its lowest ever number in the 545-member Lok Sabha. The BJP and its smaller alliance partners took 194 seats but remained at least 75 seats short of a majority. The BJP lost a chance at sustained government, resigning after merely two weeks when it was clear that it could not overcome a vote of no-confidence because it simply did not have a majority. Characterized widely abroad and at home as the "Hindu Nationalist" party (a label worn proudly within India), the BJP faced unease about secularism and concern regarding the future course of relations with Pakistan. The party leader, Atal Bihari Vajpayee, tried to reassure non-Hindus that there would be no discrimination on the basis of religion, region, caste, or class. However, the victorious celebrations of the more militant Hindu organizations were in sharp contrast to the sober language with which Vajpayee tried to reach out to minorities. Some of the excess was a likely consequence of the fact that this was the first ever national chance for the BJP and its supporters, coming in from decades of politics on the right without easy access to power. Nonetheless, the BJP president, A.K. Advani, who sat out the election because of indictment in a kickback scandal (which also touched Narasimha Rao) and who was the main mover in the razing of the Ayodhya mosque—which led to the largest Hindu-Muslim riots since partition, resulting in thousands of Muslims dead—was expected to play an important role in any government. Vajpayee's freedom of action was curtailed by some of the election promises of the BJP, which called for, among other items, the end of the special constitutional provisions for the states of Jammu and Kashmir; repeal of the special code of laws for Muslims governing marriage, divorce, and inheritance that even the British had left intact; the declaration and deployment of a full-fledged nuclear weapons capability; and a tough stance on global disarmament before India would sign on to any limited agreements, such as the Comprehensive Test Ban Treaty (CTBT). The BJP government did not get good press abroad despite several attempts to put together a government that would last. Neither the induction of a Muslim as the minister for foreign affairs nor assurances that the government would seek the best of relations with Pakistan helped the government. A series of statements aimed at reassuring the world that economic liberalization was here to stay and that India welcomed investments in consonance with its priorities in the fields of technology, power projects, and telecommunications; and the appointment of Jaswant Singh, a widely respected and well-known leader, as the minister of finance was not sufficient to sustain support for the government. Furthermore, despite Vajpayee's personal commitment to consensus and secularism, many believed that he would not be able to control the extremist elements within his party.

When the BJP gave up its efforts after two weeks, the next party in line was the United Front, which consists of a 13-party coalition of center and leftist parties with H.D. Deve Gowda, the former chief of the southern state of Karnataka (which includes Bangalore, the Silicon Valley of India), as prime minister. In 1989 a center-left alliance had ruled in India—but only for 16 months before the Congress Party came back to power for a five-year term. In 1996 the United Front coalition was sustained by the explicit support of the Congress Party, which offered its bloc of votes in order to help Gowda with votes of confidence in parliament. This exercise itself made it painfully clear that Gowda is in need of the Congress Party, which cannot form a government on its own but can bring one down.

The new government proclaimed itself to be a truly regional phenomenon with a preponderance of southerners, marking a break with the northern upper-caste prime ministers who traditionally have held power. The new prime minister quickly repeated the mantra that economic reforms are permanent and that India would continue its drive for foreign investments. He offered to continue India's existing foreign policy and quickly assured the United States that there would be no change on Pakistan and nuclear weapons, the two issues to which Washington seemed most sensitive. But the 1996 democratic process demonstrated that issues of diversity and regional resurgence were more important to voters than those of a national agenda.

Preparing to enter the 21st century, India appears to be in the throes of a coalition age where politics is determined not by one or two main parties with representative strength across the nation but by a plethora of regionally specific parties. While the BJP and its allies and the Congress Party have the most votes in the Lok Sabha, none has the strength alone to form a government. While the United Front can form a government with the explicit support of the Congress Party, it has virtually no experience at the national level to lead and govern India.

The 1996 election can be characterized as the latest of a number of "abnormal" events. In particular, the last three elections—the one in 1980, brought on by the collapse of the Janata government; the one in 1984, in the aftermath of the assassination of Indira Gandhi; and the one in 1991, following the assassination of Rajiv Gandhi—swept in the Congress Party even as an ever larger number of local leaders prepared to challenge Delhi. In the past, Indian states were treated by federal governments simply as extensions of federal power where the states were forced to do Delhi's bidding. However, the 1996 elections demonstrated a reversal of this pattern.

Despite the Congress Party's defeat, Rao remained as head of the party until September 1996. At that time he was forced to surrender his leadership. He was also charged with fraud and corruption—an unexpected end to a long and distinguished political career.

India's free press mirrored the performance of the political system and its leaders. Representing a variety of regions and interests, the press is dynamic and noisy. National newspapers regularly voice the concern of many Indians that the political system is failing to cope with the needs of the weak and the disenfranchised. High costs of elections and budding scandals are a part of the daily diet for Indian readers. The merits of economic liberalization are actively debated in the media, as are a host of problems, such as mass poverty, burgeoning population growth, an education system under stress, high defense expenditures, the costs of economic liberalization, and restive provinces. There is also extensive coverage of international news. At times, the coverage of news about bilateral relations with the United States and India's relations with smaller neighbors has been generally critical, which makes any attempt to improve relations that much more difficult.

The role of the Indian press in providing an outlet for a variety of opinions and as a vehicle for accountability of the political elites is almost unparalleled in the developing world. For Americans trying to understand India, a free and active press is something familiar in a sometimes unfamiliar world. Despite occasional excesses, the press has become a vibrant part of Indian democracy.

PAKISTAN

The political history of Pakistan has been vastly different from that of India, with basic issues of governance left largely unresolved. The task of creating a new nation with a distinct identity was complicated by the early death of Pakistan's two founding fathers, Mohammad Ali Jinnah and Liaquat Ali Khan. The separation of the country into two wings bridged by a thousand miles of India and the unwillingness in West Pakistan to let democratic norms rule caused political polarization and eventually led to war and the formation of Bangladesh.

Throughout its history, Pakistan has grappled with tensions between civil and military institutions. The very nature of partition, and the worry that India did not accept it, led to a greater sense of physical vulnerability and an emphasis on the role of the military in managing the political system. As the political elite grappled with establishing the new state, it did so under a sense of siege. Often it failed to provide the leadership that would create consensus between the provinces and across the ethnic and class divides.

Delay in agreement over the constitutional structures until 1956 meant that the political system was in a constant state of flux after Liaquat Ali Khan's assassination. There was little consensus within governments that fell in rapid succession. Even after the constitution was promulgated, parliamentary majorities were lost within a matter of months. National governments were changed, and there were difficulties in the provinces as separate entities were merged into "one unit" to create greater balance in the relative weights of East and West Pakistan. Inept governments and failed policies helped the first Pakistani commander-in-chief, General Ayub Khan, win a surprising amount of support for his declaration of martial law in 1958. For the next ten years, Ayub ran the system with and without martial law. By the end of his rule in 1969,

Pakistan had lived through its first two decades of independence without a clear blueprint for government and had survived a major war with India.

Poor political performance led to a constant search for scapegoats, such as the military, the bureaucracy, the landowners, the "22 families" who were identified as the economic elite, the immigrant "muhajirs," the East Pakistanis, and others. Failures were always someone else's fault. Each of these scapegoats suffered through a period when it was accused of being the main roadblock to national survival. The most dramatic of these periods was the rift between the two wings of the country starting with the December 1970 election. The polarized results had severe consequences for the future of Pakistan.[4] The eastern wing became Bangladesh, with India supporting the secessionist sentiments fueled by the brutal treatment of the population of East Pakistan by the Pakistan army. The Indian army liberated Bangladesh, defeating Pakistan's proud military.

Zulfikar Ali Bhutto, who had served as the foreign minister in the Ayub cabinet and left to form the Pakistan People's Party (PPP) in 1970, came to power in 1972 vowing to defend democracy. During his years in power, 1972 to 1977, the PPP edged out the opposition parties, such as the Muslim League and the National Awami Party, dismissing them in two provinces where they governed. Unlike neighboring India, where occasionally the state governments were also dismissed, from an early date the center in Pakistan was more intrusive in state affairs. Pakistani political parties were mostly not viable institutions on their own.[5] Arrest and harassment of the political leaders neutralized the parties, which seldom had a second tier of leaders.

As the performance of the political leaders faltered, the British-trained elite civil service bureaucracy began to fill the gap. In the constantly shifting political hierarchy of the period from 1947 to 1958, someone had to assume the day-to-day governing responsibility. The civil service soon began to rule on behalf of the political leaders. In contrast to India, in Pakistan there was a sense that the bureaucracy was critical to the new state and that the political elite's inept performance rendered it unfit for leadership.

The military fed the superior attitude of the civil servants, as reflected in the response of General Ayub in the 1958 martial law decree. Ayub inducted key civil servants directly into the small group that was put in place to govern Pakistan. Such open recognition institutionalized the view of the bureaucracy as somehow being totally above the political fray. Worse still, it removed the civil service from accountability to the political leadership in the nation's formative years. By the time that accountability was demanded in the mid-1970s, nearly 30 years had gone by and there was a long list of grievances. In the ensuing confrontation between the political leadership and the civil service, the nation was the loser. Subsequently, an almost irrational backlash against the civil service took much of the guts out of the system. As the first order of business after the Z.A. Bhutto years, an emasculated civil service moved to protect itself against further political assault rather than to offer up a sound scheme for governance.

Under threats of military intervention, elections have not always been a means for political change. Bhutto had fought (and won) the 1970 election as an outsider. By the time of the 1977 election, he had greatly concentrated authority in the chief executive. Thus when there were charges of fraud in the election, the blame was laid at his doorstep, as all authority within the PPP rested with its leader. The opposition, sensing victory as the PPP admitted to irregularities in 20 to 25 of the 155 seats it won in the National Assembly, insisted on new elections. Recrimination brought the system to a political impasse, and once more the military moved in. Chief of Army Staff General Zia-ul Haq became president after dismissing the Bhutto government, arresting the former prime minister, and declaring martial law without even suspending the constitution.[6] Zia did not return the system to civilian institutions as he initially promised. As he held on to power with the help of the bureaucracy, he sought legitimacy by trying to transform Pakistan into a more Islamic state. Toward that end, he pressed for the return to Islamic values that had guided the formation of the country and vowed that Islamic principles were to be the "cornerstone of the policy" of his government.[7] In December 1983 Zia held a carefully orchestrated referendum in which he asked for approval for the Islamic direction he was taking. It was announced in advance that approval would mean that the country had confidence in the president and thus authorized him to start a five-year term. After receiving a 60 percent approval vote, Zia felt vindicated even though opposition parties charged him with fraud, since the referendum did not specifically ask for his election to a five-year term. But in 1983 the opposition was weak, and the Soviet invasion of Afghanistan and the ensuing war left the government in a stronger position to deal with challenges on the domestic front.

By 1985 calls for greater participation had increased. Zia hoped that the National Assembly, which he had carefully revived on the basis of nonparty elections, would join him in further Islamicization. Yet there was no consensus on the precise role of Islam in national politics and the role of those who would interpret such law. Among the critics of the *shariah* bill and the constitutional amendment empowering the religious courts to rule on the validity of the laws were women's groups. Representing the active, urban, and well-educated sector, they strongly objected to the bill because it challenged the Family Laws Ordinance of 1961, which had provided for certain rights in case of divorce and inheritance and legislated 16 as the minimum age for females for marriage.

Although Zia put in place some measure of civilian-elected government in 1985 through his hand-picked prime minister, Muhammad Khan Junejo, real power lay with the president, who had retained the chief of army staff position. This allowed him to govern through both civilian and military institutions.[8] Zia had the additional advantage of being a familiar figure to the United States, as he had been responsible for U.S.-Pakistan joint policy against the Soviets in Afghanistan. Even with Junejo nominally in charge, Zia retained control over Afghan policy. With the U.N.-sponsored talks on Afghanistan in progress, close coordination between the governments of Pakistan and the United States was essential. Junejo had greater say in the domestic arena. His foreign policy expertise was limited, as appeared painfully clear in his official visit to the White House in July 1987 and his meeting in New York with President Reagan that October.

Throughout its history, a great deal of debate in Pakistan has focused on whether the country was better suited to be governed by a presidential or a parliamentary system. Each has been tried without a clear verdict on its efficacy. The bicameral legislature was made up of weak institutions—a 237-member National Assembly and an 87-member Senate—with power residing in the office of the prime minister and the president. In the triumvirate of Pakistani power—the president, the prime minister, and the chief of the army staff—the last has been the most influential.

The conduct of foreign policy has been even more closely managed than domestic policy. A handful of advisors have assisted the chief executive, particularly since those with a longer tenure in office—such as Ayub Khan, Z.A. Bhutto, Zia-ul Haq, and Benazir Bhutto—have all been particularly interested in foreign policy and have used personal advisors and a small foreign service to carry out the policy. That pattern did not change with the death of President Zia in a plane crash in August 1988. However, his replacement, President Ghulam Ishaq Khan, a former civil servant, stayed in office until November 1993 and was less open to discussion with the United States on key issues.

Benazir Bhutto started her second tenure as prime minister in 1993, articulating a vision for social and economic change. She listed three priority areas: the economy, energy, and a reduced rate of population growth. She continued economic liberalization launched by her predecessor, Prime Minister Nawaz Sharif, and succeeded in attracting American and other investment to Pakistan. Her policies in the social sector had limited impact despite her stated commitment to a social action plan that singled out health, women's education, and population planning. In particular, Pakistan's annual population growth neared 3 percent, higher than that of its South Asian neighbors, such as Bangladesh, and there has been a regresssion to a 90 percent rate of illiteracy among women.

Lacking a majority, she put together a coalition government. She came in with support from the traditional centers of power, the army and the bureaucracy, and even had the chance to put in her own man, Farooq Leghari, as president. The second term was thus expected to be different from her first, when she appeared unsteady and her powers as prime minister were carefully circumscribed by the president and the army. What then went wrong within three years?

First and foremost, it was the intractability of the problems of the Pakistani political system. The fragmentation of politics meant that the normal give-and-take that underwrites political interaction was absent. The ruling party and the opposition parties have very little to do with each other in this system of political governance. The party in power disposes, while the opposition opposes. Under Bhutto, the National Assembly, where there is normally debate on legislation, was reduced to acting as a clearinghouse for announcements regarding the government's agenda rather than being the focus of legislative action. Few bills were enacted, there was little debate of consequence for much of the tenure of the Bhutto government. Despite the fact that Pakistan has had democratic elections and popularly elected governments, once in office, the leader has often adopted an autocratic model of decision-making. The stronger the government, the less inclined it generally has been to engage in consultation with the opposition at the center or in the provinces. Benazir Bhutto's government followed this pattern even as she was well received at home and abroad. Neither she nor Nawaz Sharif had earlier reached out across the political divide. Thus neither gave the opposition a stake in the system. For Pakistan's political leaders, a parliamentary form of government has meant that each political leader sees the collapse of the party in power as an immediate gain for the opposition rather than a prelude to a national crisis.

Second, Bhutto's style did not encourage broad-based consultation. There was a band of favorite advisers who were close to the prime minister and ruled on her behalf. Even so, there were a large number of ministers, ministers of state, advisors, etc. whose apparent reason for existence was not to add to the quality of governance but to collect on the perks of office. There were some exceptions, but they were few and far between. In the meantime, the discretionary revenue available to the government was greatly reduced by the twin demands of defense and debt servicing, which absorbed well over half of government revenue. Thus, the distance between rhetorical promises and performance widened.

Third, lack of consensus fed alienation from the system that was even more pronounced in the provinces. The exclusion of the Muhajir Qaumi Movement (MQM) from the 1993 election meant its disenfranchisement. Representing the "*muhajirs*," i.e., those who migrated to Pakistan from India and are mostly based in Karachi, this party ran into problems with the Bhutto PPP. The latter continued to have its stronghold in the Sind province, of which Karachi—the national financial center and Pakistan's only port—is the largest city. The MQM raised anti-Bhutto rhetoric and asserted control over parts of Karachi. Bhutto branded the leader of the MQM, Altaf Hussain, a terrorist, and he fled to the United Kingdom, from where he continued to control the party. Declaring that the movement simply represented a law-and-order problem, Bhutto unleashed the law enforcement agencies to tackle the issue and would not enter into a political dialogue regarding the basic issue of power-sharing. By the time that some political talks were started in mid-1995, over three thousand lives had been lost and there seemed to be little prospect for any deal. In the meantime, financial activity was slowed and the government suffered from the ability of the MQM to lay siege to large parts of the city at will. In bringing some of the chaos under control, actions of the government led to charges of heavy-handed dealings and killings under supervision of the law enforcement agencies.

Fourth, events in Karachi also alienated people around the country, who saw a breakdown in law and order and a rising tide of crime that touched nearly everybody. Lawlessness was increasingly attributed to the aftermath of Pakistan's efforts during the war in Afghanistan. Pakistanis blamed the prevalence of guns and their use in crime on the days when their country served as a conduit for the Afghan Mujahidin. Along with drugs, which brought growing addiction as they were smuggled from the tribal areas bordering Afghanistan, guns changed the nature of life in the cities. Increasingly, governments in power were held responsible for the deterioration in the quality of life experienced by most people, who felt truly unsafe in their own homes. When Murtaza Bhutto was assassinated in a police ambush outside his house in Karachi on September 20, 1996, people were shocked that it could happen to the brother of the prime minister and that it could happen in cold blood at the hands of the very agencies that were said to be guardians of the state.

Fifth, the breakdown of institutions in Pakistan occurred over time. This downward trend accelerated during the Bhutto years when she was accused of ignoring the traditional role of the existing institutions, particularly those dealing with governance. The judiciary and the bureaucracy, the traditional mainstays of the system, were given no role or were tampered with to make them impotent. Coupled with a nonperforming legislature, the effect on the political system was telling. Instead, the control exercised by the husband of the prime minister created a parallel government without accountability. Growing corruption fed by a lack of accountability became the hallmark of a government that had come into power in 1993 full of goodwill and was exhausted by November 1996. There was a national sense of relief when the president dismissed the Bhutto government on November 4, 1996. It seemed at the time that there was no other way of ending the sad chapter that was Benazir Bhutto's second attempt at leadership in Pakistan.

Sixth, by mid-1996, Pakistan was near economic collapse. Charges of extensive looting of the national exchequer were accompanied by tampering with the economic figures, to which the World Bank and the International Monetary Fund (IMF) took great exception. Pakistan was put on a list as being the second-most-corrupt country in the world by an outside source, which was widely cited within Pakistan as an indication of how badly the Bhutto government was handling affairs. Greater transparency was demanded by the IMF, which sought direct oversight before entertaining Pakistan's request for funds to meet the severe economic shortfalls. The country was essentially bankrupt. Bhutto's journey to the United Nations in the midst of the escalating economic crisis in September 1996 did not bring relief. By the time she returned home, it was clear to her detractors that the old charm, which had in the past worked with the West, particularly with the United States, was wearing off. Her inability to get a meeting with President Clinton was cited at home as indicative of Washington's disillusionment with her rather than a function of the tight agenda before the U.S. elections. The fact that Asif Zardari, Bhutto's husband, continued to serve as minister for investment in the government only made it harder for the prime minister to deal with much of the criticism and to capture the initiative vis-à-vis her critics. Thus she found herself between the proverbial rock and a hard place. If she disowned his actions, it meant she did not control what had gone on in her own family. If she did not, it demonstrated that she was party to her husband's misdeeds. Bhutto, however, felt it was a conspiracy against her that allowed the criticism to mount rather than an aftermath of failed policies.

After three years in office, the problems facing the Bhutto government were many. The embattled prime minister dug in and faced her critics. When asked by this author just days prior to her dismissal from office why she still cared to fight on when the burden had become so crushing and, indeed, the writing was already on the wall, she answered: "because parliamentary government is important to me and I must see the country through to the completion of the term of a duly elected government." The first part of the answer did not seem surreal to her! Clearly, she had become even more out of touch with reality than one had thought.

Bhutto counted on Farooq Leghari, the man she had put in as president, to continue to be loyal to her. His decades-long association with her and the PPP was seen as the best guarantee of the support for her government over its entire tenure. In her first term, she had chafed at the controlling hand of Ghulam Ishaq as president. The second round was to be different. Once in office, however, Leghari found it difficult to continue his loyal support as things unraveled, and the prime minister refused to follow serious advice from him. As Pakistan moved toward bankruptcy, there was a crescendo of voices calling for elections or dismissal. Bureaucrats, long ignored, except the favored ones, went to the press with tales of horror about the Bhutto government. With the free press in Pakistan, these stories soon became public. The constitutional divide that Zia had built in as the eighth amendment gave the president a share of power. Leghari had not exercised these powers because he was part and parcel of the PPP and had been a junior colleague of Bhutto. Yet the constitution gave him the authority, and the supreme court upheld his right to play a significant role, should he deem it essential. As Bhutto got locked into a variety of struggles, from economic collapse of the country, to the murder of her brother, to the challenge from the right, which organized sit-ins in front of parliament to demand her dismissal, to the failure of institutions, Leghari came under a great deal of pressure. The political opposition leader, Nawaz Sharif, mended fences with Leghari and asked that elections be called to determine the will of the people. In this charged atmosphere Bhutto accused the president of conspiracies against her and her family. In the last weeks of her government, Bhutto was increasingly cut out from some of the key decisions as the president moved against a government isolated from the public and proclaimed that it was the most corrupt in Pakistan's history. When she was finally removed from office, Bhutto claimed that the action was unwarranted and unconstitutional. Her challenge was thrown out by the supreme court.

Under the terms of the constitutional process invoked by Leghari in his dismissal of the Bhutto government, fresh elections must be called within 90 days. A process of accountability was also promised. Immediate focus turned to cases of corruption against Zardari and his collaborators in the government, including some in the bureaucracy and the security services. Those found guilty were expected to be barred from future elections. Some felt that the process should be wider and include those in the previous government of Nawaz Sharif, which also had its share of scandals and whose tenure was also marked by cases of corruption. Others thought that both Bhutto and Sharif should be disqualified in order to prevent a seesaw political power game. There were even those who thought that the best option was the continuation of the interim government until political accountability could be enforced, the economy was put on a sound footing, the institutions were strengthened, and a long overdue census in Pakistan corrected representation patterns. According to such a view, only then would elections make sense.

The carefully mapped out Zia plan for sharing constitutional power has been the subject of debate as each successive prime minister has tried unsuccessfully to engage the opposition to repeal the provisions of the eighth amendment that empowered the president to challenge the authority of the chief executive. There is little to indicate that there will be any major change anytime soon.

The role of the army and the chief of army staff has been central to the Pakistani set up. Whether or not elections are held on schedule, that fact is unlikely to change. Leghari's move could not have taken place without the acquiescence of the military. Army units were deployed in strategic locations prior to the dismissal during the night of November 4, 1996, and Bhutto was confined by the military to the official residence for a brief period. Prior to Leghari's move, the army chief had acted with restraint in his dealings with Bhutto. She was said by most who dealt with her to have refused to take advice, even from those who wished her well. At the same time, many admit that Benazir Bhutto is at her best when she is challenged and it is not inconceivable that someday she could be back in power.

The February 1997 change of government in Pakistan will not resolve the urgent problems facing the country. Institution-building, return of law and order, social problems, revival of political discourse, an end to corruption, economic solvency, some coherence in the decision-making process, and accountability and transparency are all issues that any government coming to power will have to deal with. Even if the political process is once again set aside and Pakistan goes into a period of martial law, the nature of the problems will remain largely unchanged. Then the military will have to find a way of dealing with all of the problems that can only briefly be postponed by an overthrow of civilian authority.

2

Foreign Policy Choices

THE COLD WAR SHAPED INDIAN AND PAKISTANI POLicy on the international scene, and its end has caused a basic readjustment in the foreign policies of both countries. Here we examine the nature of the regional and international system involving India and Pakistan and the choices that face them in the next few years.

BACKGROUND

Perhaps the harshest legacy of the British raj in South Asia was the manner in which the empire ended in the subcontinent. Earlier British hesitation was replaced in 1947 with an almost indecent sense of haste with which boundaries were drawn, leaving a myriad of problems in their wake. As independence dawned, Indian leaders were unconvinced that the new state of Pakistan could survive and saw the partition as a negation of the very essence of India. Pakistani leaders were convinced that India would not allow their separation to continue and felt an acute sense of injustice in the way that Kashmir was awarded to India.[1] Believing that a fair hearing from Britain was impossible, Pakistan looked elsewhere for friends. The onset of the Cold War provided an opportunity as India and Pakistan sat astride a region contiguous to the Soviet Union. With the success of the communist revolution in China in 1949, geostrategic considerations governed U.S. relations with both India and Pakistan.

Washington, which had no sense of colonial guilt and presumed that good relations with both India and Pakistan were possible, approached the subcontinent with hopes of establishing strong bilateral ties. India, distinguished from other newly independent states by its size, population, and promising democracy, was a natural candidate for American interest. But Washington underestimated Indian pride: its leaders wanted a greater acknowledgment on the world stage than would come to it simply from being the lesser ally of yet another major Western power. Aware that containing communism was a goal of American foreign policy, India felt that it could play a constructive role in the rapidly expanding East-West competition and wanted to probe the possibilities on all sides. The Non-Aligned Movement (NAM), of which India was a cofounder, was a direct result of the desire to stay out of the Cold War. Moreover, the NAM gave India its own arena for action, an arena seen by the United States as decidedly pro-Soviet, especially as India often voted with the Soviet bloc at the United Nations.

In their messianic desire to contain communism, some Americans, such as John Foster Dulles, could not conceive that "neutrals" could have any positive value. Nehru appeared arrogant to many American policy makers, who tired of his lecturing on the virtues of restraint in international relations and his criticism of the United States as supporting colonialism rather than self-determination.[2] The presence of the Pakistani option may have enhanced Washington's short-tempered reaction to Indian policy as Pakistan offered tangible benefits to the United States. Pakistanis were quick to point out that in their view restraint was far from certain in the policies India itself followed vis-à-vis its smaller neighbors. In the 1950s, political and strategic ties expanded rapidly between Pakistan and the United States. On the political front, Indian policy often clashed with that of the United States. The unwillingness of India to condemn the Soviet invasion of Hungary in 1956, for example, upset Washington as being blatantly hypocritical. The U.S. reaction, in turn, influenced Indian attitudes toward American policy, which later made it easier for Washington to support Pakistan when the latter cried foul against Indian policy.

Alignment also bore certain costs for Pakistan in diminished influence with the developing countries for whom India had a particular appeal. Several of these, such as Egypt and Indonesia, which were close to India, did not welcome Pakistani ties to the United States and sought to limit Pakistan's role as a fellow Islamic state in the councils of developing countries. Assistance that came from the American connection provided Pakistan with compensation for its diminished role in the larger Islamic bloc. While proclaiming neutrality, the first prime minister of Pakistan, Liaquat Ali Khan, cultivated links with the United States as early as 1950. Being wary of China subsequent to the Korean War, and recognizing Pakistan's potential as a listening post against communism, the United States in 1953 offered support for defense. The offer was welcomed since falling jute and cotton prices made it impossible to meet the costs of defense domestically. Pakistan signed the Mutual Defense Treaty with the United States in May 1954, giving the latter access to the airbase in Peshawar, close to the Soviet and Chinese borders, and giving Pakistan its best chance to mount an expanded and more modern defense. Membership in the Baghdad Pact, later known as the Central Treaty Organization (CENTO), and in the Southeast Asia Treaty Organization (SEATO) gave Pakistan access to America's friends in the West and in the East and access to American weapons and training. But membership also had negative consequences. Claiming that the alliances had altered the situation, India repudiated its pledge to the United Nations for a plebiscite in Kashmir. Perceiving the American alliances as an affront, the Soviet Union punished Pakistan with its veto on Kashmir in the Security Council. The Soviet Union vetoed resolutions dealing with the Kashmir plebiscite nearly one hundred times between 1954 and 1964 (the 1948 resolution was passed with Soviet concurrence), effectively putting the issue in a deep freeze at the United Nations. In December 1955, Soviet leaders Nikita Khrushchev and Nikolai Bulganin declared in Srinagar that "Kashmir was an integral part of India." The 1959 executive agreement between the United States and Pakistan provided Pakistan additional weapons for its armed forces. From the mid-1950s to the mid-1960s, U.S. arms assistance amounted to $650 million.[3] This made Pakistan one of the largest recipients of U.S. military assistance in the Third World. Much later and with considerable hindsight, Pakistanis believed that their leaders had neglected opportunities elsewhere by remaining so firmly in the American camp. However, at the time, with the fixation on India and its need for a powerful friend, Pakistan enthusiastically rushed to the U.S. corner.

The price for alignment was steep, and Pakistan paid it willingly, despite potentially serious consequences. Allowing the United States to use its facilities to launch spy planes over the Soviet Union created problems when one such plane was shot down over Soviet territory in May 1960. The threat of retaliation against Pakistan by the Soviet premier could not shake Pakistanis' belief that their relationship with the United States was a key element of national interest that had to be protected. In turn, the Soviets became suppliers to India of aircraft and armor, two items of particular importance in Indo-Pakistan wars, along with the other hardware that India requested.

As the Cold War unfolded, the foreign policies of India and Pakistan were adjusted and fine-tuned. One such shift resulted from the Sino-Indian border war of October 1962, which affected India's relations with the United States. Perhaps the fact that John F. Kennedy was president had something to do with the alacrity with which the United States responded to the trauma of the China war. Kennedy greatly respected the Indian prime minister, Jawaharlal Nehru, and understood the stakes of a debacle for Nehru at the hands of the Chinese. Washington was also genuinely sympathetic to India's fear of deep Chinese gains and the inadequacy of Indian military preparedness. In seeking American assistance, Indian leaders sought a careful balance between the need for it and the need to protect the remnants of Indian nonalignment.[4]

While the border war did not last long, it reminded India that the American option might be useful.[5] The United States was pleased in 1962 by its ability to help India in a limited but timely fashion. Yet the new relationship between India and the United States distressed Pakistani leaders, who felt that they had not been consulted. However, American efforts to consult Pakistani president Ayub Khan prior to offering India assistance were stymied by Ayub's making himself unavailable at a critical moment. Ayub dismissed Washington's assurance that the arms would not be used against Pakistan as reflecting U.S. naïveté and ignorance regarding Indian intentions and the nature of the Indo-Pakistani conflict.[6] Minimally, Ayub wanted Kennedy to press India for a solution to the Kashmir dispute, arguing that it would free up Indian forces in the north to concentrate on the China front. Kennedy, worried that Pakistan might in fact open up a second front for India in Kashmir, asked Ayub for a "no-war" pledge. Ayub Khan reminded the Americans that as early as November 1959, he had offered a joint defense pact to India and that Nehru had turned down the offer with a caustic "defense against whom?" Nonetheless, as Nehru worried about Pakistan's strong pro-China position, Kennedy dispatched the assistant secretary of state for Near and South Asia to Pakistan and urged restraint in Kashmir. Pakistan did oblige but ended up feeling betrayed that the United States did not reward such restraint.

These events had a dramatic impact on the domestic political scene in Pakistan. It brought Zulfikar Ali Bhutto, the new foreign minister, into prominence within Ayub Khan's cabinet. Bhutto used the 1962 episode to criticize what he termed the one-sided nature of the relationship with the United States. He called for a greater balance in Pakistani foreign policy, involving a warming to both China and the Soviet Union. Ayub Khan agreed with this proposal; the result was the March 1963 border agreement with China that effectively made China a party to the Kashmir problem. Ayub Khan moved further by improving economic, cultural, and scientific relations with China and in forging new ties to the Soviet Union. These actions did not please the United States, which was increasingly enmeshed in the Vietnam War. Characterizing the Pakistani move as "an unfortunate breach of free world solidarity," the Johnson administration showed its pique by canceling a small loan for the expansion of the runway in Dhaka, in what was then East Pakistan, because of the agreement for the Pakistani national carrier to fly to China, and scolded Pakistan for "opening up the window" to the world for China.

At the time of the second Indo-Pakistani war over Kashmir, in September 1965, India had recovered from the 1962 trauma and had put its friendship with the Soviet Union back on track. War came amid Pakistani miscalculations that an uprising along the Indian part of the line of control in Kashmir was possible with only limited help from Pakistan. Bhutto had convinced Ayub Khan that the attack would be confined to Kashmir, a "disputed" territory. Ayub believed that the Pakistani position would never be better and that Kashmir would not be given the promised self-determination option by India, nor would the United States force India to give it that option. He calculated that Pakistan could deal with the Indian response in Kashmir. Instead India struck massively across the international border in the Punjab, where Pakistan was vulnerable. The possibility existed that other fronts could open along the 2,000-kilometer border between India and Pakistan.

As had been the case previously with Southeast Asia, it took a war to focus U.S. attention on the subcontinent. The United States initially worried about the possibility of Chinese intervention, and Washington joined Moscow in urging an end to the hostilities. Once the Indians threatened Pakistani territory, the Pakistani ambassador to the United States officially requested assistance. The secretary of state, Dean Rusk, concluded after carefully examining the bilateral agreement with Pakistan that the United States was unable to help. Noting that Pakistan had not consulted the Americans prior to the infiltration in Kashmir that set off the Indian attack in the Punjab, Rusk said that the United States was "being invited in on the crash landing without having been in on the take-off."[7]

Two days after the war started on September 6, 1965, the United States suspended all arms aid to both India and Pakistan. This signaled U.S. unhappiness with the conflict and was an attempt to bring it to an early end. The strategy worked. Pakistan, which had become almost entirely dependent on American arms, recognized that it had to terminate the war quickly. Initially the Soviets agreed to join in the arms cutoff to India (which was more reliant on Soviet sources for supply), but it rescinded the ban a week later, on September 17. Pakistan touted the Soviet action as showing the steadfastness of the Soviet Union (toward India) and the unreliability of the United States toward its friends (Pakistan). However, the Americans and the Soviets cooperated at the United Nations to try to end the war. The Soviets offered their good offices, and Indian and Pakistani leaders met at Tashkent on January 4, 1966. The declaration issued there on January 10 restored the status quo ante and gave the Soviet Union a new image as a peacemaker in South Asia.

After the 1965 war, India and Pakistan stepped back from open conflict but were unwilling to move toward rapprochement. The United States was fully engaged in Southeast Asia. India and Pakistan were preoccupied with their respective domestic agendas. Whenever their officials met at international forums, Kashmir surfaced as an irritant; Pakistan reminded the world of an unfulfilled promise for self-determination that had yet to be delivered, and India demurred. Washington had little enthusiasm for involvement with the quarrelsome neighbors, and the American relationship with Pakistan continued to fray.

Although the United States had lowered its profile in the subcontinent, Pakistan still had a key role in American foreign policy. President Richard Nixon and Secretary of State Henry Kissinger used the Pakistani channel in their secret efforts to normalize relations with the People's Republic of China. Kissinger's clandestine visit to Beijing in June 1971 was routed through Islamabad, and Pakistan provided the cover of his feigned illness for the duration of the American delegation's presence in Beijing. Pakistan was more than pleased to help both its friends reach accommodation and expected that certain benefits would accrue from its efforts. India, still suspicious of China and mindful of the 1965 war with Pakistan, cast a watchful eye on events unfolding in East Pakistan and was stunned by the American announcement that Kissinger's trip had led to a decision to normalize U.S.-China relations. News of the Pakistani role caused even greater discomfort as Delhi worried that there was more to the U.S.-China relationship, perhaps even involving further Chinese actions against India.

Washington welcomed the December 1970 elections in Pakistan as marking an end to martial law and prolonged periods of military rule. But the elections left a politically polarized country, with the eastern wing under the Awami League led by Sheikh

Mujibur Rahman and the western half under Bhutto's PPP. Under established rules, Mujib, who had received more votes, should have been the new prime minister. Instead, with Bhutto's encouragement, General Yahya Khan launched a brutal attack on the civilian population in East Pakistan, which led to the third Indo-Pakistan war and the end of Pakistan as a country with two wings. By mid-July 1971 the Indian prime minister, Indira Gandhi, was openly referring to the former East Pakistan as Bangladesh. Washington's attempts to help Pakistan by backing the appointment of a civilian governor and by assisting with refugee resettlement (the latter was especially important, since the government of India said that the flow of huge numbers of refugees from East Pakistan into India was a cause for Indian involvement) came to naught. When Kissinger went to Delhi, Mrs. Gandhi urged that all aid to Pakistan be stopped, believing that U.S. aid to Pakistan in the shadow of the Bangladesh crisis was inappropriate. The request drew the following response from Kissinger: "Indian leaders did not think it strange that a country which had distanced itself from most of our foreign policy objectives in the name of nonalignment was asking us to break ties with an ally over what was in international law a domestic conflict."[8]

Lines were further drawn in August 1971, when India and the Soviet Union signed a 20-year treaty of friendship. Both countries stressed that the treaty was not a military alliance and need not worry those "who are genuinely interested in the preservation of peace in Asia and the entire world."[9] Article IX of the treaty pledged that the two would refrain from assisting any third party in the case of a conflict with one of the contracting sides. The timing of the treaty reflected the concern Nixon's China opening had created in Delhi. Both Moscow and Delhi were happy to further cement their relations as events unfolded in South Asia. Doing so bought Delhi insurance (given the million-strong Soviet troop presence on the Sino-Soviet border) against Chinese military support for Pakistan in a war with India. The Soviets seemed pleased to demonstrate that China could not prevent India's defeat of Pakistan in the war over Bangladesh, at a time when Pakistan had believed that its close relationship with the United States (and Nixon and Kissinger's assurances) would bring support if it got into serious trouble. The United States acted to prevent the collapse of West Pakistan. Watching the movement of the U.S. carrier USS *Enterprise* into the Bay of Bengal on December 15, 1971, Indians worried that it might enter Indian waters even as India accepted the cease-fire on the following day.[10] However, the Soviet Union, India, and Pakistan did not view the naval movement as a serious threat. Nevertheless, India deemed the move a "tilt" in American policy and unwarranted protection for Pakistan.

CHALLENGING THE SOVIET UNION IN AFGHANISTAN

The next time the United States focused intensely on the subcontinent came in the aftermath of the December 1979 Soviet invasion of Afghanistan. The source of the trouble was not a South Asian country, as in the past, but instead America's main rival. The invasion closely followed the fall of the shah in Iran at the hands of a deeply anti-American group and fed Washington's concern that the tide was turning against the West in the region. The seizure of the embassy in Tehran and the public humiliation of Americans held hostage there left a legacy of negative feelings in the United States regarding the region in general coupled with a fear of Islam in new Iranian garb. In November 1979 the United States was dismayed at violence against American assets in Pakistan as the embassy was burned by an unruly mob, with police making very little effort to stop the action. Nevertheless, in its last months in office, the Carter administration came to realize that with the Soviet invasion of Afghanistan (under the flimsy pretext of defending the existing regime), Pakistan had replaced Afghanistan as the buffer state in South Asia.[11]

The issues of peace and security came together as the United States sought ways to reduce Soviet pressure on Pakistan. The move toward assistance had already been initiated before the end of the Carter administration. The Reagan administration increased aid on September 15, 1981, with a $3.2 billion five-year program divided equally between economic and military assistance. It was a huge commitment. A serious effort to move the Soviets out of Afghanistan required a strong Pakistani role as a front-line state, which could not be built without a major aid program. The key element in the U.S. calculation was the belief that bringing about Soviet withdrawal from Afghanistan was both essential and possible. Pakistan took the lead in the diplomatic arena in mounting the challenge at the U.N. General Assembly in successive years to call for the withdrawal of Soviet troops and the return of Afghan refugees—some 5 million—who had fled their country, with 3 million going to Pakistan and another 2 million to Iran.

Washington expected Delhi to strongly condemn the Soviet invasion. Mrs. Gandhi, who had just come back into office in January 1980, was said to be leaning in favor of a condemnation, as had the Janata Party, which went out of power in January, but official Indian statements reflected the preferences of their bureaucratic drafters and did not denounce the Soviet move. Upon receiving a strong reaction from the United States, India made more critical comments regarding Soviet occupation of Afghanistan. India did not welcome the close coordination between Pakistan and the United States. Further, the new situation meant that not only would Pakistan's military capability be upgraded significantly but also that China would become an important player. The United States did not believe that the assistance given Pakistan was a threat to India, and Washington tried to design an assistance package to supply only such arms as were needed for the war in Afghanistan. Pakistan seized the initiative to publicize international disapproval of Soviet actions. India, however, could not afford to condemn such an important friend and thus chose quiet diplomacy.

Washington recognized that the arms package had to be substantial enough to enable Pakistan to withstand Soviet pressure, that there had to be a concessional element to the program, and that it had to be a multiyear package because of Pakistani concerns about U.S. reliability. The package was a combination of grants and loans for the security assistance portion along with some foreign military sales credits at treasury rates.

The economic assistance package was a mix of economic support funds, development assistance, and PL-480 foodstuffs starting in 1982 at $150 million and rising to $325 million in 1987.[12] These funds were for priority areas such as health, narcotics control, energy, agriculture, and infrastructure improvement. Washington hoped that the funds would help support policies of economic liberalization in Pakistan.

Beyond the actual amounts dispensed under the agreement, the joint effort against Soviet occupation of Afghanistan revitalized the U.S.-Pakistani institutional links, which had atrophied since the 1950s. Pakistan emphasized its new nonaligned status and announced that the assistance package did not ask for any actions that would be at variance with that status. The United States made clear that the new agreement assumed that Pakistan would support American objectives on nonproliferation and narcotics control.

India, Pakistan, and the United States all recognized that the Soviet invasion of Afghanistan had changed the nature of U.S. engagement in the subcontinent even though at no previous time had the United States sought a close relationship with Kabul. Afghanistan had been free to cultivate a special relationship with the Soviets with the underlying assumption that the Soviet Union would respect Afghan nonalignment.

Yet Afghanistan's nonaligned status had been compromised well before the Soviet Union invaded. The 1978 coup d'état in Kabul that brought the Khalq faction of the Afghan Communist Party to power did not initially elicit a strong negative response from the United States. Only when the American ambassador, Adolf Dubbs, was assassinated in February 1979 in the presence of a Soviet advisor did Washington appear to recognize the growing difficulties in Afghanistan.

The United States understood that there was a legitimate Soviet interest in the region. Subsequently, even while asking for the withdrawal of Soviet forces and the restoration of Afghanistan's nonaligned status, the United States made no attempt to absorb the country into its own sphere of influence. Such a calculation accepted the limited nature of U.S. influence in the area and the small probability that Washington could sustain the interest of succeeding administrations in subcontinental affairs. In any case, Washington also recognized the difficulty of playing any significant role in the Afghan conflict without the help of a regional partner, and Pakistan was the only logical choice. U.S. policy objectives in Afghanistan matched many that Pakistan supported; of these, Soviet withdrawal was central.

The United States insisted on complete Soviet troop withdrawal within a short time. Pakistan was content with the American position in part because it believed that U.S. staying power was limited. But Pakistan feared the consequences for its borders and the possibility of a two-front threat should Soviet presence outlast American involvement. Self-determination was another objective of U.S. policy. The United States felt that the free expression of Afghan will in an impartially administered manner was the obvious rejoinder to the Soviet occupation. Details of such an exercise of free will were to be worked out subsequent to Soviet withdrawal. Pakistan had its own ideas; of course, so did the resistance leadership. Additional U.S. objectives, including the restoration of Afghan independence, nonalignment, and the return of refugees, also suited Pakistan.

Initially, India did not react negatively to these American objectives, although Gandhi made the point that providing arms to Pakistan would inevitably lead to additional Indian defense expenditures, diverting funds from development and creating tensions. As late as 1985, the Indian leader said, "It is not for [India] to comment on what the U.S. does to Pakistan, except on the nuclear issue."[13] The difficulty was that American objectives required massive support for the Afghan resistance movement through Pakistan. The U.S. provision of economic help and security assistance to Pakistan as a corollary of the effort in Afghanistan increasingly irritated India. The earlier Indian suspicions surfaced again along with talk of a "special" U.S.-Pakistan relationship.

Washington understood the importance of India to the Afghan effort. As India was a friend of the Soviet Union, its policy on Afghanistan counted with Moscow. India did not support Soviet policy because it could not remain indifferent to the invasion of a small nonaligned nation. However, Delhi was careful at the U.N. General Assembly to refrain from joining in the overwhelming public condemnation, one of very few non-Communist states to do so. This greatly disappointed the United States.

The Reagan administration tried to improve relations with India even as it launched its revived security relationship with Pakistan. Past attempts to get away from the zero-sum game vis-à-vis India and Pakistan had failed. This time the president felt that the stakes were high, and the chance to reduce Soviet power offered an incentive for the United States to improve relations with India and Pakistan simultaneously and to use that improvement to better their relations with each other.

Washington policy makers sought three goals. Minimally, the United States desired better U.S.-Indian ties because they could help in preventing the opening of a two-front confrontation for Pakistan. Second, the United States aimed for improvement in relations between Washington and Delhi substantial enough to be used to better Indo-Pakistan ties. Third, the United States emphasized that American support for the expulsion of the Soviets from Afghanistan was important for regional security and a key element of the Reagan Doctrine.

By 1984, a steady stream of official American visitors regularly traveled to Pakistan in support of the Afghan effort. The visits incorporated stops in India to discuss a growing list of issues. All American conversations at the senior level actively encouraged good relations between India and Pakistan. Throughout the Reagan years, South Asian leaders had unusual access to the top leadership in Washington. The president himself was actively involved, meeting officially with Indian prime ministers and with Pakistani leaders on four occasions. These meetings reflected the important role India and Pakistan were seen to be playing in the maintenance of peace and security in South Asia and in working for a Soviet withdrawal.

Recognizing that technology was the most promising driving force for an improved relationship with India, the United States and India concluded a memorandum of understanding in November 1984 setting forth the rules for the flow of technology. The Indian list of requirements was long and featured products with advanced U.S. technology. Some items thus had to be ruled out, but the administration tried hard to accommodate requests that were at the upper end of technology but did not jeopardize American nonproliferation goals and policy restrictions. The visit of Prime Minister Gandhi in June 1985 and his discussions with President Reagan and Vice President Bush helped make the case for continued presidential and vice presidential involvement. Gandhi understood that U.S. controls made it difficult for India to obtain an unlimited range of dual-use items but was forthright about the fact that India needed the most advanced American technology.

Personal chemistry between Reagan and Rajiv Gandhi was exceptional. The American president liked Gandhi's approach to the development of high technology for India and his willingness to seek American help. Reagan also took Gandhi's pragmatic desire to go to the best source as reflecting the changed international environment; no longer could the Soviet Union maintain its privileged place in Indian foreign and economic policy. For an administration challenging the very existence of the Soviet system, Gandhi's shift away from Moscow represented a welcome change. In his dealings with Gandhi, Reagan did not minimize the important role that Pakistan played for the United States as a front-line state in the fight against the Soviet occupation of Afghanistan. Rather, the United States continued to encourage better Indo-Pakistan ties, something that Gandhi and Zia told Reagan they also favored. Responding to the U.S. call for normalization, both leaders stressed in their respective meetings with American officials that they understood the advantages of a better relationship. Zia emphasized that arms purchases from the United States protected Pakistan on its Afghan front. He argued that Kashmir was not the issue since the Soviet occupation of Afghanistan made any move in Kashmir, with its attendant possibility of opening a second front, unthinkable.

The Reagan administration believed security assistance had four goals: it enabled friends to work for peace and democratic reform; it provided a tangible means for the translation of rhetoric into action; it bolstered friendly forces in areas of vital interest to the United States; and it brought stability to regimes under stress and denied "cheap victories to those who profit from regional turbulence."[14] Under these criteria, Pakistan's case demonstrated U.S. seriousness in dealing with a country directly threatened by the Soviet invasion of Afghanistan. Believing that steadiness was the key factor in the U.S. regional security posture, the United States committed itself to a multiyear effort in Pakistan. Further, security assistance was seen as a means of helping reconciliation between India and Pakistan. Such a policy rebutted the age-old argument that the United States had to favor one country or the other at any given time.

Despite broad support for the policy on Afghanistan within Congress and the administration, some asked whether these commitments exceeded U.S. capabilities and even questioned the role of security assistance. The Reagan administration worked hard to secure congressional backing for its subcontinent policy, undertaking a major effort to keep key members informed. This was a practical necessity, given the large annual appropriations that were involved. Delegations from the Senate and the House traveled regularly to India and Pakistan to meet with the leaders, to get a firsthand look at the effectiveness of the effort against the Soviets in Afghanistan, and to evaluate the administration's claims that the countries supported mutual confidence-building measures.

Pakistan's nuclear policies also came under scrutiny, along with the administration's efforts to slow down the nuclear weapons program by supplying sophisticated conventional weapons. Congress accepted the argument that there was a need for U.S. assistance to Pakistan if the Soviet Union was to be challenged in Afghanistan. But congressional concern about the nuclear issue inevitably meant that Pakistan's failure to provide acceptable guarantees about its nuclear program would provoke congressional strictures. These came as amendments to the assistance legislation requiring a cutoff of U.S. aid to Pakistan should it engage in activities such as enrichment, reprocessing, manufacture, or illegal acquisition of materials for the nuclear program, including violating American export laws.[15] Senators Stuart Symington, John Glenn, and Larry Pressler and Congressman Stephen Solarz put their names on legislation that called for penalties if Pakistan undertook these prohibited actions.

Besides spending major sums to challenge the Soviet occupation of Afghanistan, the Reagan administration consistently showed Soviet leaders that the occupation was a serious impediment to the improvement of bilateral U.S.-Soviet ties. The centrality of that message carried over to the U.N.-supervised talks on Afghanistan. In round after round, the Soviets were urged to withdraw their forces, allow self-determination for the Afghans, and permit the return of refugees.

Throughout the decade-long effort to contain and then expel the Soviets from Afghanistan, Washington operated from the premise that the Soviet occupation was only a first step for Moscow policy makers, a step driven by their presumed desire for power projection and the warm-water ports of the Persian Gulf. Reacting to the prospects of such a scenario, the Carter Doctrine of 1980 had declared that: "An attempt by any outside force to gain control of the Persian Gulf region will be regarded as an assault on the vital interests of the United States of America and such an assault will be repelled by any means necessary, including military force."[16] Thus the Persian Gulf region acquired an importance previously allocated only to Europe and Japan. In keeping with the declared American interest, Washington announced the upgrading of U.S. power projection capabilities through the creation of a Rapid Deployment Force, which later became the Central Command headquartered at MacDill Air Force Base, Tampa, Florida.

In the search for support in the joint effort against the Soviets in Afghanistan, China was a natural first choice. Beijing's interest in preventing further expansion of the Soviet empire and a history of close ties with Pakistan meant a shared interest with the United States. Given U.S. unwillingness to be openly identified as a weapons supplier to the Mujahidin, China became the main supplier of weapons that were indistinguishable from their Soviet counterparts.[17]

The United States also coordinated its strategy on Afghanistan with key Muslim states, especially Saudi Arabia and Egypt. Pakistan was a partner in the enterprise and maintained its own bilateral links with the Islamic bloc as it sought broad assistance for the Afghan effort and isolation of the Soviet Union. The United States marshaled its resources to provide the wherewithal for the Afghan resistance to mount a "jihad"—a holy struggle or war—against the Soviet Union. The Afghan Mujahidin—a term used even by the United States to describe those who engaged in jihad—proudly proclaimed the battle to be a holy one. Each successive resistance leader who journeyed to Washington or received American officials in Pakistan repeated that the jihad required the expulsion of Soviet forces from their country. Such statements received favorable reaction from senior American officials and wide coverage in the American press.[18] As a principal provider of the means for the jihad, the United States shares the blame for the ascendancy of the "fundamentalists" in Afghanistan. Only after the Soviets left in defeat and some of the very same "fundamentalists" began to appear threatening to American interests elsewhere did the United States objectively acknowledge some of the costs of its Afghan strategy.

As noted, the escalation of help to Pakistan and the Afghan resistance ("freedom fighters" was Washington's preferred term) was coupled with concrete steps to continue the dialogue with India. By the time of the second Rajiv Gandhi visit to Washington, in October 1987, a steady stream of Indian requests for technology had been considered and many had been approved. Among these was a Cray XMP-14 supercomputer, although given the time it took to obtain the 1987 presidential approval of the request and arrange for delivery, the machine barely rated its description as a "supercomputer."

The supercomputer request was preceded by a number of confidence-building steps between India and Pakistan, all of them actively encouraged by the United States. The United States was pleased that the Gandhi-Zia meeting of December 1985 had led to an agreement not to attack each other's nuclear facilities. That agreement meant that the most dangerous aspect of the countries' policies—their nuclear programs—were in common focus even though the two leaders disagreed on the nature of their programs and were less than open with each other about the sites where nuclear fissile material was stored. The White House considered the agreement important because of the danger that either side's attack on a nuclear facility might lead to general war. In a 45-minute private meeting, the two leaders dealt with a variety of other irritants. They resolved to discuss a pullback of forces at the Siachen Glacier and to restart the negotiations for a no-war pact proposed by Pakistan and a treaty of peace and friendship proposed by India. They also directed work by the joint commission to oversee the improvement in trade, travel, and other problems.[19]

American willingness to be positive toward India was reinforced by the Indo-Pak agreement not to attack each other's nuclear facilities, first suggested by the United States in September 1985,[20] and other moves that were, in the words of Gandhi, a "first step towards restoring confidence in each other." Proof came in the clearance of the GE F-404 engine for the projected Indian light combat aircraft. Gandhi quickly asked for further concrete evidence of the new relationship by pressing the supercomputer request. He believed that the first approval would be difficult but that once it was granted, India would routinely receive subsequent approvals.

Sensitive to American concerns that the computer not be utilized for any defense-related activity, India installed it at the meteorological institute in Delhi. Given the importance of monsoon forecasting and related research for the Indian economy and agriculture, the computer was favorably received. The request was also part of the developing Indian dialogue with the Pentagon; Defense Department officials began a series of exchanges, the capstone being the visit of Secretary of Defense Caspar Weinberger to India in October 1986. Bangalore, India's high-technology capital, was added as a stop for the visit, and Weinberger was shown India's domestic capability along with its ability to keep American and Soviet technology separated—a major concern for U.S. officials in Washington who had to approve technology transfer requests. The sale of the Cray was handled carefully to meet the U.S. need for protection and the Indian desire to proceed quickly. A safeguards regime was painstakingly worked out between the computer company and the Indians so that U.S. concerns were met. The seriousness of the issue was reflected in the fact that the president personally approved the sale after listening to the critics and only after India had agreed to an American protection regime for the computer. The Indian request for the more advanced XMP-24 was downgraded to the XMP-14 model, a decision Gandhi reluctantly accepted. The assumption was that if India abided by the spirit and the law of the agreement and the protection regime worked, the XMP-24 request would be considered later.[21] At the time there were fewer than 200 supercomputers in the world; India's acquisition of one meant that it had achieved world-class research status. The Cray became the symbol of India's new relationship with the United States, as it was the first such sale to a nonally.

Once the U.S. government had taken the lead, American companies and individuals accelerated joint ventures with their Indian counterparts. By 1987, 25 percent of the joint ventures in India came from the United States. Two-way trade was expected to be in excess of $6 billion, up from the $4 billion average for the previous four years, at a time when a second assistance package for Pakistan, which included a list of defense items for the Afghan war, was under discussion. Gandhi publicly denied any U.S. pressure on India to compromise its national interest and asserted that the nature of U.S.-Indian relations had changed since 1985. He said that the improvement had occurred despite U.S. military assistance to Pakistan and the American refusal to give India the level of economic assistance and technology that it requested. Gandhi went on to say that India wanted good relations with all its neighbors, including China. Toward that end, he was willing to expand the Indian-Chinese negotiations beyond the difficult border issue and to travel to Beijing.[22] This same message was delivered in his October 1987 meetings with Reagan during a cordial working visit to Washington. The United States was supportive of the Sino-Indian normalization, hoping that the action meant further weakening of Indian ties with the Soviet Union. Reagan also hosted a private lunch for Gandhi, which the Indian delegation greatly appreciated.

The Gandhi visit was followed by preparations in Washington for the Reagan-Gorbachev summit, scheduled for December at the White House. Afghanistan remained on the agenda, but the focus shifted after a dramatic November announcement by the official Soviet spokesman, Gennadi Gerasimov, that the Soviets could withdraw their troops in 7 to 12 months. Although this time frame was still long by American reckoning, the Soviets appeared to be getting serious about a withdrawal. At the summit, Reagan shocked Gorbachev by clarifying that U.S. assistance to the resistance would continue despite any Soviet agreement to withdraw. In other words, the old adage "trust but verify" that Reagan liked to quote was applicable, and the United States would watch the pace of the Soviet withdrawal and subsequent Soviet actions before terminating assistance to the Mujahidin. After the summit, Gorbachev offered a 12-month withdrawal period, provided the United States also agreed to stop military and financial assistance to the Mujahidin. The United States pressed for a shorter timetable for withdrawal and asked that a proportionately larger number of troops be withdrawn initially. Gorbachev indicated that the Soviet Union was finally prepared to opt for a neutral and nonaligned

Afghanistan, probably in recognition of the fact that eight years of occupation had failed to bring Afghanistan firmly into Moscow's orbit. Reagan, in responding to the changed Soviet attitude, acknowledged that the United States would continue to insist on actual verification of Soviet withdrawal. Subsequently, he moved to approve the agreement whereby the Soviets undertook to pull out of Afghanistan following the Geneva Accords of April 1988.

Toward the end of the long road to Geneva, Gandhi invited Zia to Delhi for talks on Afghanistan. However, Pakistan was unwilling to give India a voice so late in the game; after all, in their view, for years India had been reluctant to actively support the joint U.S.-Pakistan Afghan strategy. The great game was coming to an end and the U.S.-Pakistan relationship was about to lose one of the central issues on which it was built: its alliance against the Soviets.

The agreement for withdrawal of Soviet troops and the transfer of power to the Mujahidin was signed by Afghanistan and Pakistan with the United States and Soviet Union acting as guarantors in Geneva on April 14, 1988. Yet, indirect negotiations went on for six years, and the Afghans' suffering continued. Signing for the United States, Secretary of State Shultz declared that "history has been made today." Pakistan and Afghanistan pledged to respect each other's sovereignty, political independence, territorial integrity, national unity, security, and nonalignment. In signing as a guarantor of the agreement, the United States noted that the Soviets had been put on notice that full compliance with the withdrawal timetable was critical. The United States retained the right "consistent with its obligations as guarantor to provide military assistance to the parties in Afghanistan. Should the Soviet Union exercise restraint in providing military assistance, the U.S. similarly will exercise restraint."[23] In his response, Zia acknowledged that the primary role in the jihad belonged to the Afghans. However, without the will and support of the United States there could not have been the rollback of the Soviet empire and the restoration of peace and stability to South Asia. The United States achieved its objectives of a speedy and complete withdrawal of Soviet troops, restoration of Afghanistan's independence and nonalignment, and a partial return of refugees. Self-determination for the Afghans, however, proved harder to implement as the Afghan leaders who were key to the process refused to cooperate with one another.

The Soviet Union completed the withdrawal of its forces from Afghanistan on February 15, 1989, ten months after the Geneva agreement.[24] At American insistence, withdrawal was front-loaded—50 percent of the soldiers would be out within the first three months in an irreversible withdrawal. President Reagan stated clearly that the United States reserved the right to continue support for the Mujahidin.[25] However, by then the essence of the Soviet state was changing and American attention began to turn from the periphery of East-West competition in Afghanistan to the core areas of Europe. Soviet exhaustion with the Afghan effort, coupled with the Soviet Union's own new outlook—expressed by Eduard Shevardnadze's public remark that the 1979 intervention was "illegal" and "mistaken"—helped the United States to sponsor Soviet integration into the world community. The Soviet-American arms control agenda that the United States sought seemed finally within reach.

One of George Bush's first meetings as president-elect was with the leader of the Afghan Alliance. The meeting signaled continuing American involvement with the Afghan situation and the expectation that existing policy would stay in place until Soviet withdrawal was completed. Bush also pledged U.S. assistance in the massive reconstruction and refugee resettlement effort that was to follow. U.S. interest in the demining of Afghanistan was particularly important as the Soviets offered no maps and were believed to be unlikely to cooperate without U.S. pressure.

The war left Pakistan with more than one lasting and troubling legacy. It institutionalized the policy of active involvement of its intelligence service (Inter Services Intelligence, or ISI) in domestic and foreign policy. Successive Pakistani leaders have been unable to eliminate this interference, although some have succeeded in reducing it. All have had to contend with the ISI's efficient machinery using its own sources of funds. The United States had helped build up the ISI to oversee the key goal of expulsion of the Soviets from Afghanistan. With that goal achieved, the ISI was able to claim credit and credibility for future actions, with or without sanction from the political leadership, and in areas where it was less than qualified.

A deterioration in Pakistan's own law-and-order situation was another consequence of the decade-long effort to arm the Afghan Mujahidin. The large-scale use of Pakistani territory by the resistance made guns a familiar item. Once introduced, arms became a part of the political culture and contributed to an upsurge in crime. Drug addiction was another growing problem in Pakistan, as the country became a conduit for the drug trade going from Afghanistan to the West. Furthermore, large numbers of Afghans remained as refugees because conditions in their homeland made it impossible for them to return.

Political turmoil with its attendant high costs continues within Afghanistan. Despite years of sacrifice and over 1 million civilian casualties as a result of the Soviet occupation, Afghans won no respite after the Soviet withdrawal. Kabul, Jalalabad, and other areas experienced even greater destruction. Loyalties changed as often as the fortunes of the several factions. Leaders like Gulbuddin Hekmetyar, whom Pakistan originally favored and whom the United States allowed to receive supplies because of their commitment to the cause and their presumed efficiency as fighters, got most of the weapons stockpiled in Afghanistan once the Soviets left. Lacking its earlier leverage, Pakistan was unable to influence any reconciliation between factions despite its desire to do so. Without political consensus, Afghanistan remained a dreaded patchwork of fiefdoms under the control of different warlords. However, despite these costs to both Pakistan and Afghanistan, the Reagan Doctrine had worked and the United States successfully used its resources to roll back the Soviet empire and reduce its influence in the Third World.

The Soviets were estimated to have spent $5 billion to $6 billion a year on the Afghan war.[26] These outlays, plus the human costs, added to the Soviet Union's exhaustion.

The end of Soviet withdrawal did not mean the settlement of the Afghan issue for Pakistan. Attempts by successive governments in Islamabad to help establish a government in Kabul failed. The battle for control by the Afghan factions led to a constant state of civil war with serious consequences for the embattled population. All of the leaders who had successfully fought the Soviets for nearly a decade subsequently turned to fight each other. At different times, Gulbuddin Hekmetyar, Burhanuddin Rabbani, Ahmed Shah Masood, and Abdul Rashid Dostum all headed governments or were parts of coalition governments, but peace remained elusive. Kabul itself suffered a great deal of destruction as warring factions sought control. A long-suffering population watched as a new phenomenon, the *Taliban* (students from religious schools; *talib* is Arabic for "student"), quietly captured large areas of Afghanistan without a fight.

Pakistani support for the Taliban, who took over in Kabul amid much fanfare in September 1996, came under increasing criticism even as Islamabad denied that it was behind their success. Instead, Pakistani officials cited their view that a war-weary Afghan populace had been happy to support the end to fighting and the return of some normalcy to their daily lives. However, once the Taliban enforced regulations requiring women to stop working, a strict dress code and other forms of control, the impact of the new order began to emerge. At the same time, the push for control in the north brought the Taliban into direct conflict with the area's powerful leaders. Having withdrawn from Kabul in favor of the Taliban, Masood, Rabbani, and Dostum took a stand that pushed the Taliban forces out of Panjsher Valley and back to the outskirts of Kabul.

The desire for control over Afghanistan meant that the Taliban challenged the warlords in charge of the provinces who were ethnically different and whose agenda set different priorities. In their control over Herat, the Taliban alienated Iran. As they sought to move north, they set off alarms in Russia and India regarding their fiery brand of Islam. Pakistan sought to bring peace, and President Leghari, along with senior officials, made a trip to the Central Asian states to seek a rapprochement and help in forming a unity government in Kabul. Pakistani policy suffered a setback as turmoil continued in neighboring Afghanistan; the Pakistan embassy in Kabul was burned to the ground during the Rabbani government in April 1996. Islamabad worried about the partition of Afghanistan along north-south lines. Western governments, unhappy with the antiwomen dictates of the Taliban, threatened an end to humanitarian assistance for Afghanistan. The ethnic Pashtoon Taliban had links with similar tribes within Pakistan, and some in Pakistan talked of the consequences for Pakistan of the Taliban entry into the politics of Afghanistan. U.N. efforts to end the fighting and create broad support for a government in Kabul have moved extremely slowly.

REGIONAL REALIGNMENT—SAARC

As Soviet withdrawal drew near, there were discussions in regional capitals about the nature of the subcontinent after withdrawal. Some, like Zia, feared that Pakistan's importance would decline even before the ink was dry on the Geneva Accords, leaving the country to shoulder the burden of refugees and armaments. The second six-year U.S. assistance package[27] was in its initial period, and it was not clear that aid would flow without the Soviet presence and threat.[28] Furthermore, new U.S. budgetary constraints were bound to endanger the country's position as the third largest U.S. assistance recipient, after Israel and Egypt. Islamabad hoped that the withdrawal would not change American interests and pointedly recalled that the Carter administration had made the same error, only to change its policy a year later at a greater cost.

The most accurate review of Indian policy during the period was made a few years later by a former Indian foreign secretary, Jagat Mehta.[29] He concluded that India's inability to participate in the search for a democratic, moderate, and nonaligned Afghanistan had resulted in the "sidelining" of India. Indian policy was based on the fact that the Soviet Union had been a tested friend, despite Indian dislike of superpower interventions in the subcontinent. By surrendering that support in the early stages of the Soviet occupation, India did not help "rescue the Soviet Union from a no-win situation." Furthermore, Mehta asserted, India's vote in the United Nations on Afghanistan had been misconstrued as justifying a big country's intervention in spite of the small neighbor's sovereignty.

Consequently, India's neighbors, some of whom already had various disputes with their large neighbor, felt the need of some regional vehicle to coordinate policy. Such an institution also could be used to further the common interest in a variety of nonpolitical fields. Thus was born the South Asian Association for Regional Cooperation (SAARC). In order to deal with Indian sensitivities that all the other members might band together against it, SAARC agreed to leave political issues outside its mandate.

When the first SAARC summit took place in December 1985, it was a new attempt to institutionalize an era of peace. In a message to the leaders assembled at Dhaka, Reagan pledged U.S. support for all regional efforts toward a secure and peaceful South Asia. The Dhaka summit was followed by a cordial Gandhi-Zia meeting in Delhi that same year at which the two leaders agreed to prohibit any attack on each other's nuclear facilities. While India and Pakistan had different approaches to the Afghan issue, apparently the two leaders felt capable of finding common ground on other issues. Announcing the nuclear agreement, Gandhi referred to the fruitful bilateral resolution of several problems, and Zia spoke of a coordinated regional approach that could bring the subcontinent into a different mode of operation.

Regional peace, however, remained illusory as escalation of strife in Sri Lanka, whose Tamil population had been fighting for autonomy since 1983, drew India in on the side of the Tamil separatists in the north. Conscious of its own Tamil population, India could ill afford to ignore events in Sri Lanka. Mounting violence and resulting casualties led Indians with ethnic links to the Sri Lankan Tamils to pressure Gandhi. Undoubtedly encouraged by such sentiment and the material help that India provided, Tamils refused to enter into any discussions with the Sri Lankan government. The Research and Analysis Wing (RAW) of the Indian intelligence agency, compounded the issue with support for the hardline Liberation Tigers of Tamil Eelam (LT TE). No solution seemed possible without Indian agreement. When the government in Colombo escalated the military pressure against the Tamil rebels with the hope of denying them food and military supplies, Indian air force planes air-dropped both, sending Mirage 2000 jet fighters and Antonov AN32 transport planes across the Palk Strait to the northern coast of Sri Lanka. Colombo criticized these Indian actions as a grave violation of Sri Lankan sovereignty but suspended its offensive. A month later, in July 1987, Sri Lanka signed an agreement with India in which the president, Junius R. Jayewardene, made concessions to the Tamil minority. For his part, in a deal that was to lead to his own assassination some four years later, Gandhi pledged to adhere to the territorial integrity of Sri Lanka and to use Indian clout with the Tamils to enforce the agreement.[30]

At the annual SAARC summit, India was not criticized for its actions in Sri Lanka.

As the war started to turn against the Soviets in Afghanistan, the much-improved Indo-Pakistan relationship underwent some severe tests. Previous actions had won both countries plaudits. The 40th anniversary of the United Nations brought Gandhi and Zia to New York for a productive meeting, the message of which was identical to that emerging from their separate meetings with Reagan: it was time for a new beginning. The American policy of offering carrots in the form of security for Pakistan and technology for the economic development of India began to resonate with these countries. The American press acknowledged that it was an effective approach.[31]

Despite Indian and Pakistani moves forward to develop better relations across a broad front, it seemed that war by miscalculation still remained a possibility in South Asia. The 1986 military exercise "Brass Tacks" sparked a serious crisis. Earlier that year, General K. Sunderji became the chief of army staff in India. As early as December 15, 1985 (at the same time as Gandhi received Zia in Delhi and signed the nuclear facilities nonattack agreement with him) at a meeting of service chiefs, Minister of State for Defense Arun Singh and Prime Minister Gandhi approved the idea of large-scale exercises. They agreed that the logical man to oversee the entire operation would be the new army chief.[32]

Perhaps in order to appeal to the hawks in his bureaucracy, Gandhi went ahead with the order for the exercises in July 1986. The size and location (which demonstrated a capacity to attack in an area below the traditional route in the Punjab) and the planned length of the exercises alarmed the Pakistanis. As the exercises proceeded, Pakistan staged its own exercise, "Saf Shikan," on the other side of the Rajasthan border from Indian forces. In the final phases of Brass Tacks, additional Indian forces from the Punjab and Haryana were moved in, feeding war paranoia in Pakistan and threatening the constituency for better relations with India. Zia called for calm, saying that India would not create a war situation and that Pakistan was keeping a careful eye on troop movements. However, he ordered an armored division in the southern sector of Pakistan to move closer to the border, a bold stroke that caught

India unprepared and generated fears of a Pakistani attack in a weakly defended area. Pakistan's air bases went on full alert and remained so for a while after the Indian exercises terminated.[33]

Scholars have hypothesized that the Brass Tacks exercise was a means for General Sundarji to test his "computer-generated Ft. Leavenworth–type concepts of mechanized, mobile warfare."[34] If so, it created a great deal of difficulty on both sides of the border and concern in the United States that escalation could spark war and wipe out the carefully built foundations for peace. The United States undertook political as well as military contacts with both governments to reduce escalating suspicions and to encourage an early, peaceful end to the respective military exercises. Eight years after the exercise, Sundarji admitted that he had not considered the impact on Pakistan. Minister of State for Defense Arun Singh later recalled that by downplaying the threat of war, failing to see Pakistan's strong reaction to Brass Tacks, and failing to keep the prime minister informed of the deteriorating situation, he may have displeased Gandhi.

The crisis was discussed at the political level at the SAARC summit in Bangalore in November 1986; Gandhi promised to scale down the current exercise. However, tension continued until early the next year. Gandhi also sought to reassure Pakistan through Egypt's President Hosni Mubarak, asking Mubarak to explain India's peaceful intentions to Zia at the Organization of the Islamic Conference summit in Kuwait. The United States also urged both parties to talk and prevent such scenarios from occurring in the future and thereby avoid further conflict. As the exercises wound down, diplomacy went into high gear. Foreign secretary talks in Delhi during January 1987 resulted in an agreement to exercise prudence and to withdraw troops from the border.[35] The United States encouraged the two sides to discuss Pakistan's earlier offer of a "no-war pact" and India's proposal for a treaty of "peace and friendship." Zia invited himself to a cricket match in Madras in February 1987, and the pace of improvement quickened as confidence-building measures dealing with notification of military exercises and use of hot lines went in to effect.

Brass Tacks had reminded Washington that even though neither Pakistan's nor India's leaders might want war, armed conflict between the two countries was a real danger. Washington worried that such escalation would have negative consequences for the war in Afghanistan and destroy its earlier work in helping to bring about Indo-Pakistan rapprochement. Hostilities also would bring the Soviets deep into South Asian affairs and force the United States once again to play the zero-sum game in the subcontinent.

As talk surfaced in Washington in 1987 about the supply of advanced warning airborne command systems (AWACS) and other sophisticated weapons to Pakistan in the second assistance package, which totaled $4.2 billion for economic as well as military assistance, Gandhi complained that such arms exceeded what Pakistan needed for the Afghan war. In his 1987 meetings with American leaders, however, Gandhi did not dwell on that theme, preferring to spend his time making the case for U.S. technology transfers to India. Yet in his statements to the Indian parliament and in press interviews, he hammered home the danger that arms escalation posed to improved Indo-Pakistan relations. This message was music to the ears of a group of Indian hard-liners in the defense, intelligence, and external affairs bureaucracies who were opposed to moving fast on normalization with Pakistan. They let the United States know of their unwillingness to make agreements with Zia (even though he had the will and the authority to make such deals) because of his "nondemocratic" credentials.

KASHMIR: A HOT PEACE

While Kashmir and its effect on U.S. policy is not the focus of this book, any discussion of the foreign policies of India and Pakistan must include some consideration of the issue.[36] A peaceful future for the region requires some way around the current impasse. Any compromise is difficult because all sides are unbending. India will not tolerate a change in the status quo and hopes that the broadening of the political dialogue through elections will satisfy the demand that the people of Kashmir be assured of full participation in determining their future. The new government in New Delhi has talked about the possibility of full autonomy for Kashmir within the context of the Indian constitution. Recent elections in Kashmir also are perceived in Delhi as having brought into power a state leadership with Kashmiri and Indian national credentials. For New Delhi the election is the alternative to the insurgency and a legitimate means to deal with Kashmiri grievances against the Indian government. Pakistan refuses to accept any such formula and doubts that elections can resolve the Kashmir issue. Neither side wants to focus on the possibility of a third option—some form of autonomy for the entire state.

Five years of active rebellion inside Kashmir has left a bitter legacy and halted the process of normalization between India and Pakistan. Islamabad is not willing to move forward on other fronts until the "core" issue of Kashmir is settled. According to the Pakistani statements, if the Kashmir issue is "resolved"—meaning through the promised U.N. resolution for a plebiscite in Kashmir—all other difficulties will be sorted out since Kashmir is the main reason for all major disagreements between India and Pakistan.

Cessation of violence by all sides, the freeing of political prisoners, and a withdrawal of paramilitary forces from the populated areas are cited as some of the preconditions for the return of normalcy to the Kashmir valley. Because of the escalation of violence, a steady flow of refugees left for Delhi beginning in 1989. These people must be allowed to return to their homes and businesses, and will require substantial compensation. To reduce the current potential for violence in the valley, the intelligence agencies of both countries must play a reduced role and weapons infiltration across the line of control must cease. Pakistan says it is not involved in arms shipments and would welcome the deployment of U.N. monitors to substantiate its claim. Political rhetoric continues to be inflammatory. India firmly believes that the only permissible negotiation must be between itself and the Kashmiris. Pakistan sees a role for itself in any outcome both because of the Security Council resolution and because of the continued Pakistani belief that Kashmiris still have an emotional tie with Pakistan. Each side wonders if arms can be laid down without some prospect of an outcome beyond a simple cease-fire.

In the last couple of years, international interest in the Kashmir issue has focused on human rights violations. India, which is estimated to have over half a million troops in Kashmir, is often criticized by international human rights agencies for violations.[37]

India admitted that there were genuine problems but claimed that these were manageable without Pakistani interference. Pakistan was criticized for aiding and abetting the uprising inside Indian Kashmir and was nearly placed on the U.S. list of states supporting terrorism for the help it rendered dissident Kashmiris.

Discouraged by the continuing human rights violations in the valley and encouraged by Clinton administration statements emphasizing the priority of human rights in American foreign policy, Pakistan decided to up the ante against India and to take the Kashmir issue to the United Nations Human Rights Commission in Geneva in 1994. There Pakistan hoped to get a resolution pointing out what it thought were egregious Indian human rights violations in Kashmir. As is often the case with serious violations, Pakistan initially sought the appointment of a special rapporteur to investigate the Indian record. At a minimum, the resolution was expected by Pakistan to move the Indian government into some form of discussion on Kashmir. Pakistan's participation was at a high level. Prime Minister Benazir Bhutto opened the discussion with an impassioned statement regarding the plight of Muslims in Kashmir at the hands of the Indian security forces. There were two major problems with the Pakistani strategy: first, Pakistan's failure to take a position of leadership in the Security Council in the early days of its membership in 1993 regarding the plight of Bosnian Muslims cost it moral credibility when speaking on behalf of the Muslims in Kashmir.[38] Second, India had a great deal more support than Pakistan had counted on. A number of key Asian countries, including China and Iran (both traditional friends of Pakistan), calculated that their respective problems with their own dissident groups, already under international scrutiny, could worsen were they to call for an examination of what India claimed to be a purely domestic matter. Furthermore, Pakistan found that the United States did not want to choose between India and Pakistan on the issue of human rights; the Americans preferred to ask Pakistan to stand down from the confrontation.

Thus, as it always has been, the Kashmir issue remains a prisoner of the domestic political scenes in India and Pakistan. Outsiders have offered a number of innovative proposals for solutions, including one that called for India and Pakistan to retake the areas under their respective control, except the valley, which would have a referendum to select sides, but neither Pakistan nor India has taken up any of these suggestions.

Pakistan has encouraged a U.S. role in seeking a solution in Kashmir since the United States is the only major power that has good relations with both countries and is capable of being an intermediary. India flatly disagrees, holding that Kashmir is entirely a domestic issue. Early Clinton administration statements acknowledging Kashmir as disputed territory and stating that the United States never accepted Maharaja Hari Singh's 1947 decision to join Kashmir to India raised a howl of protest in India. The United States backed down somewhat and returned to its earlier rhetoric calling for a bilateral attempt under the Simla agreement to sort out the future of Kashmir. When asked about the potential for a solution of the Kashmir question, Secretary of Defense William Perry said during his visit to India in January 1995 that the United States urged both sides to resume talks on the subject despite the absence of any set of proposals to reduce tensions.[39]

THE COLD WAR ENDS

Neither India nor Pakistan expected that the Soviet Union's withdrawal from Afghanistan would be followed quickly by the end of the Soviet state and its breakup into the constituent parts of the Commonwealth of Independent States (CIS). India was a member of the Security Council in 1991 and 1992 and saw—firsthand—the changed behavior at the United Nations, where a pliant Russia went along with American leadership in responding to the Iraqi invasion of Kuwait. With the demise of the East-West struggle, India's traditional policy of nonalignment at the United Nations meant little, and its position of leadership, once seemingly secure, had to be earned anew.

Over the decades, myriad connections have been established between India and the Soviet Union. With the latter's demise, India was deprived of its main source for weapons. On the economic front, agreements critical to the Indian economy for the import of Soviet raw materials at favorable rates and the export of Indian goods had to be renegotiated. Essentially overnight, Delhi had to move to replace the overall agreement with a series of separate ones or face a shutdown of some industries. Indian policy makers scrambled to catch up with the reality of a changed international environment in which a true and proven friend no longer focused on India or provided special economic arrangements.

Five years earlier, however, Indian economic policy had already begun to shift the focus of its future pattern of development. Gandhi had spoken widely of his expectations regarding the role of U.S. technology. In a speech to the International Chamber of Commerce in Delhi, he underscored his intention to continue focusing on economic reform to improve India's dynamism and to encourage other countries to look for joint ventures with it. Similarly, India wanted greater access to American markets. The United States indicated its willingness to help but pointed out that there were lingering problems with Indian quota restrictions, steep tariffs, and questions of intellectual property rights. By May 1989, the United States considered putting India on the list of worst offenders under section 301 of the 1988 Trade Act. The Indian government agreed to discuss intellectual property rights and market access issues, but with little enthusiasm. It considered the entire trade act a bullying exercise by a superpower. The Indian commerce minister, Dinesh Singh, lamented that "we will have to live in such an unequal world."[40]

India's development of its missile capability also brought U.S. criticism. Even at the height of Indo-Soviet cooperation, India had always maintained an independent missile manufacturing capability. Following the collapse of the Soviet Union, India moved toward self-sufficiency in many areas, including missiles. The "Agni," its first intermediate-range ballistic missile, was due for its first test in 1989, at about the same time as the U.S. administration and Congress were criticizing Indian trade practices. The Bush administration, worried about missile proliferation, mounted pressure against the prospective test firing of the 1,600-kilometer-range missile with its capacity to carry conventional, chemical, and nuclear warheads. The test was postponed amid further charges of unfair behavior by the United States against India.

The tempo of Indian utilization of U.S. technology quickened. An Indian satellite, INSAT-1D, was launched from an American Delta launch vehicle in May 1989 under a commercial agreement. Positive signs of cooperation helped deflect attention from the negative aspects of the U.S.-Indian relationship such as the missile or trade issues. The relationship survived the negative publicity resulting from the disastrous gas leak at the Union Carbide factory in Bhopal. In the charges and countercharges that flowed from the accident, few expected that any compensation ordered by the Indian Supreme Court would be sufficient. After the $470 million award, the press noted that it was larger than awards commonly made by Indian courts and would help provide immediate relief to the claimants. Fears of retaliation against greater U.S. economic involvement as a result of the Bhopal disaster proved unfounded.

In 1987 the United States acknowledged India's "pivotal" role for peace and security in South Asia.[41] After India's relations with its smaller neighbors, Sri Lanka and Nepal, deteriorated, the term implied American acceptance of India's leading role in South Asia. Indian leaders looked to the United States as a key partner in technology and trade, perceived as the real levers of power. The enhanced relationship led to the beginning of cooperation in defense production and military-to-military contacts. The United States continued to support Indian access to multilateral sources of funding.

The return of democracy to Pakistan in late 1988 coincided with the withdrawal of the Soviets from Afghanistan and the end of the Cold War. President Bush had known Benazir Bhutto from his days as the U.S. permanent representative to the United Nations, when the senior Bhutto was Pakistan's foreign minister. In a letter congratulating Bhutto on her electoral performance, Bush stated that he foresaw that as the leader of the PPP and armed with the largest bloc of votes, although not a majority in the 1988 elections, Bhutto would go on to form the government. Coming from the president-elect of the United States, this rapidly became a self-fulfilling prophecy.

Once in office, Bhutto needed the assistance of multilateral institutions. The IMF came through with $800 million as a loan, although it asked for higher taxes and a cut in spending. Thus the new prime minister's first moves were a series of unpopular measures that made the absence of any real legislative agenda even more telling. Her problems were compounded by the gender divide in which, with a low overall per-capita income of $350, males are middle-income and females are ultrapoor. A population growth rate of over 3 percent added to the difficulty in making economic progress. Bhutto felt pressured by the conservatives who supported the continuation of all ordinances, some of which worked against women, as well as from women activists who looked to the country's first female prime minister for some signs of progress on their grievances.[42]

On the foreign policy front, during her first term in office Bhutto took several positive steps to normalize relations with India. She even publicly acknowledged (in an interview with the BBC) that she had made it possible for Rajiv Gandhi to deal with extremists in the Punjab by denying them safe haven in Pakistan. Defense secretary talks regarding the 20,000-foot-high Siachin Glacier in Kashmir nearly succeeded in bringing about the withdrawal of Indian troops from that flash point. Bhutto's first foreign trip after taking office was to Saudi Arabia, where she performed the Ummra pilgrimage and met King Fahd. She journeyed that year to China to cement the traditional strong ties with that country. Her visit to the United States brought a great deal of favorable exposure. She recognized that the nuclear issue was likely to divide the countries and publicly told a joint session of Congress that Pakistan neither had nor would develop nuclear weapons. She pledged cooperation on the narcotics front, understanding that the continuation of the six-year American assistance package required this. She asked for 70 additional F-16 fighter aircraft and put down $658 million in Pakistani funds to cover half the eventual cost.

The ultimate success for Pakistan was the withdrawal of the Soviets from Afghanistan even as critical problems remained unresolved. As Zia was fond of saying: "It takes a superpower to check a superpower."

As Afghanistan receded into the background, the sense of mutual need between Washington and Islamabad once again reverted to a relationship where Pakistan needed the United States more than the latter needed the former. Moreover, as we shall see in the next chapter, Pakistan's reactivation of its nuclear program in early 1990, despite repeated pledges by Ms. Bhutto to the contrary, led to a cutoff in all U.S. assistance on October 1, 1990. These developments dealt a major blow to U.S.-Pakistan relations.

After the cutoff of American assistance, Pakistanis argued about the action and claimed that the nuclear program was not the real issue; rather, the end of the war in Afghanistan had altered U.S. priorities. Critics of American policy included General Aslam Beg, who, as chief of army staff, understood, as did the president of Pakistan, the consequences of the mandatory application of American legislation in the event of any escalation in Pakistan's nuclear policy. Beg had played a critical role in the pursuit of the Afghan policy and had been an important interlocutor with the United States on the subject. However, he became extremely critical of the United States during the Gulf War. Beg argued that Pakistan had been a trustworthy and reliable ally in the American containment policy but now needed strategic cooperation with Iran. In Beg's words, "Throughout the Cold War, Pakistan had tried to be helpful; consider the case of the Sino-American normalization, the Afghanistan crisis, the Persian Gulf War, and so on. With the end of the Cold War and the importance of economic interests in the new world order, the United States has been hasty in downgrading its relationship with Pakistan." Beg and other critics were not convinced by the American rejoinder: that Pakistan had disrupted the relationship through its nuclear program. On the contrary, Beg strongly believed that the program had not fundamentally changed but rather that earlier the United States had chosen to overlook the details in order to use Pakistan against the Soviets in Afghanistan.[43]

While earlier claims that the United States had slowed Pakistan's armament program by supplying only conventional weapons may have had some credibility, that rationale sounded increasingly threadbare to the U.S. Congress. Islamabad presumed that 40 years of friendship would allow the U.S.-Pakistani relationship to continue to support the interests of each. While there was little left in the assistance pipeline, American concurrence was essential to the delivery of the large assistance package from the Aid-to-Pakistan Consortium[44] and multilateral lending institutions.

In 1993, as the country moved to elections after the dismissal of the Nawaz Sharif government, Pakistan requested $2.6 billion. Economic reforms and improvement in economic performance were expected under Moeen Qureshi as interim prime minister. Foreign exchange reserves increased to $876 million from the $200 million in the previous year, and Pakistan was on the road to economic recovery.

In the early 1990s, India took two actions that impressed American policy makers. The first was the decision by the Rao government to change its economic course. The emphasis on liberalization and privatization was music to American ears. It not only made sense, it also meant that India had at last acknowledged the failure of its public-sector policy, a holdover from the halcyon days of the socialist experiment. The second was New Delhi's normalization of relations, in the real sense of the term, with Israel.[45] In the heyday of nonalignment, India showed solidarity with Egypt, a cofounder of the movement, by limiting ties to Israel even as a consulate was maintained in Bombay.[46] Sensitivity regarding its large Muslim population of 120 million also had reinforced that policy, especially as India found itself put on the defensive by Pakistan within the Islamic bloc. However, such a policy made less sense as Arab-Israeli peace moved forward and several key members of the Islamic bloc moved to normalize their relations with Israel. The Indian action seemed particularly bold in the face of Pakistani policy toward Israel, which remained even more conservative than that of Saudi Arabia. With the upgrading of relations to the ambassadorial level and the opening of an Indian embassy in Israel, Delhi moved quickly and sent P.K. Singh, one of its most dynamic career foreign service officers, as the first ambassador. Singh had overseen the relationship with the United States as joint secretary in the external affairs ministry in the late 1980s and was respected in Washington.

India then encouraged greater American attention to the danger of Islamic fundamentalism, a warning that was already being heard in the United States. The involvement of veterans of the Afghan war against the Soviets in other venues, such as Kashmir, was a troubling legacy with consequences for Indian secularism. Delhi pointed to the arc of Islamic countries, including Iran and Iraq, both considered rogue states by the United States, and argued that the growing importance of radical religious elements meant potential trouble for the United States and India. The Indian argument resonated with the United States, where the end of the Cold

War and the demise of communism in Moscow had weakened the rationale for cooperation with Pakistan. Also because of Pakistani support for the rebellion inside Indian Kashmir, the United States seriously considered putting Pakistan on its list of countries supporting terrorism. Only a deft performance by the government in Islamabad in dispatching an associate of Prime Minister Nawaz Sharif to Washington for talks blocked that decision.

The history of U.S. relations with India and with Pakistan illustrates the difficulty inherent in a common approach to two countries that have hostile relations. As one of the two superpowers in the bipolar world of the post–World War II period, the United States was unable to ignore the subcontinent for long. For geostrategic reasons, the United States was inevitably lured into involvement in the region during periods of crises and near crises.

India's multifaceted foreign policy required a greater degree of freedom than was possible if it had a close relationship with the United States. Nor was India willing to offer the benefits of close alignment that Pakistan presented in the form of a base from which to listen in on the Soviets. However, cooperation with Pakistan did not mean that the United States was willing to participate in Pakistani ventures, a lesson Islamabad learned with dismay during its 1965 war with India.

Despite the difficulties, from time to time the United States tried hard to maintain good relations with both India and Pakistan. Success came about in the shadow of the Soviet occupation of Afghanistan. American commitment to South Asia increased during the 1980s. Improved relations also meant that Washington made a serious attempt to help improve relations between India and Pakistan.

Personalities weigh heavily in the development of relations between the United States and India or Pakistan. Particularly in Pakistan, the United States looms large in all issues of consequence. The United States has made known its preference for an elected government in Pakistan even as it collaborated with its military rulers. During periods of civilian rule, with its attendant chaos, some Pakistanis have credited the American emphasis on elections and the threat of sanctions by multilateral lending institutions with keeping the weak political system in place and the military from taking over. These same individuals, however, acknowledge that elections and civilian governments in Pakistan have not necessarily been good guarantors of either human rights or of adequate economic performance.

The fact that the United States and India are democratic countries makes it easier to focus on the positive aspects of their relations after the end of the Cold War. Already India has gained as the United States backed away from its earlier calls for human rights groups to have access to Kashmir. Washington now urges that India and Pakistan follow their agreement at Simla in its emphasis on a bilateral solution for Kashmir. However, the Clinton administration has added the caveat that "the wishes of the people of Kashmir" be taken into account. After a rocky start, the administration focused on India and sent its third ranking defense department official, who is one of its brightest senior diplomats, as ambassador. The results have been dramatic for U.S.-Indian relations, proving once again that in U.S. relations with South Asia, personalities count.

The visit of the American secretary of defense, William Perry, to India in January 1995 resulted in the signing of a military accord between the two countries that was to launch "a new era in our security relations."[47] Signing on behalf of the government, Shankarrao Chavan, the home minister, acknowledged that the accord was an attempt to forget the past in defense matters and make a new beginning. Indian leaders no doubt recognize that nothing will undermine their priority twin pillars of trade and technology as much as another war in the subcontinent.

In contrast to the situation in Pakistan, Indian options narrowed with the end of the Cold War. With the collapse of the Soviet Union, India lost a good friend and a strong supporter. Without the Cold War political standards with which to fault Indian foreign policy, the United States increasingly felt comfortable with India. American concern about the destabilizing effect of regional conflicts should encourage countries of the subcontinent toward better relations with each other. Indo-U.S. relations are of primary importance in the new scheme of things. With its democratic traditions and its size, India is bound to be the main concern of American policy in the region. Both Pakistan and India should also benefit from the continuing improvement of Indo-U.S. ties so long as the United States does not craft its entire South Asia policy to suit New Delhi. An India interested in the maintenance of regional cooperation is likely to flourish. Equally the United States can ill afford to overlook the benefits of collaborative efforts in the subcontinent.

3

Nonproliferation: A Mirage

THE UNITED STATES CUT OFF ITS ECONOMIC AND MILitary assistance to Pakistan on October 1, 1990, in accordance with its policy of inflicting heavy penalties on any country developing a nuclear weapons program. By that year the United States had concluded that despite a slowdown in the nuclear program, the president could not certify to Congress, as required under the Pressler amendment, that continuation of the assistance would contribute significantly to stopping Pakistan's acquisition of a nuclear weapons capability.[1] The imposition of the amendment reflected the fact that American efforts to keep Pakistan within the circle of nonnuclear weaponized states had failed. How had all this come to pass? The story of nuclear nonproliferation in South Asia follows.

PREVENTING PROLIFERATION

The United States demonstrated the awesome power of nuclear weapons at the end of World War II and later sent the "Atoms for Peace" exhibit around the world. Both these actions are remembered in the subcontinent as seminal, and both leaders and the general population saw in the nuclear programs a route to modernization. In energy-short South Asia, a program to provide nuclear energy made sense. The first burst of scientific activity on the nuclear front was in pursuit of the energy option. India and Pakistan made the case for nuclear energy, pointing out their growing needs and their shortage of domestic energy sources. The West cooperated by providing training and technical assistance to both countries. While Indians and Pakistanis seriously pursued nuclear power generation, they also held the underlying belief that mastery of nuclear technology went hand-in-hand with being a first-class power. This belief was a major incentive for scientific and government support of nuclear programs in both countries.

India and Pakistan were early and active members of the International Atomic Energy Agency (IAEA), serving on its board of governors. Both had active research establishments, and India had a sizable pool of scientific talent from which to draw for the nuclear energy programs and to send to the West for further training. Furthermore, India's scientists were active members of the international science community.

As it has done in other areas of the world, in South Asia the quest for a nuclear weapons capability followed the emergence of political and strategic difficulties with hostile states. India's border conflict with China in 1962, followed by China's acquisition of nuclear weapons capability in 1964, stimulated the growth of India's nuclear weapons lobby. China was a major Indian concern because India was well within the reach of the Chinese arsenal. According to the group advocating a nuclear weapons option, India's national security and its importance as a key nonaligned state demanded that it join the nuclear club. The Indian program demonstrated its viability with its first nuclear explosion in 1974. Despite the small size of the explosion, India had crossed the psychological and technical barrier, and arms control specialists in the West recognized the country's new status. External controls in the form of legislation were deemed unnecessary, given the Indian decision at the time to forgo development of a full-fledged nuclear weapons option.

The scientific base for the Indian civil program began at the Tata Institute of Fundamental Research as early as 1944 (three years before independence). In 1946 the Atomic Energy Research Committee was formed under the chairmanship of Homi Bhabha, a renowned theoretical physicist and a fellow of the Royal Society. The Atomic Energy Act was passed in April 1948, and the Atomic Energy Commission established in August that same year. The successor, the Department of Atomic Energy, was created in 1954, reporting to the prime minister. The institutional framework for the nuclear research program was thus in place by the late 1950s.

The Indian program stressed self-reliance, which meant an early emphasis on education and training. The Bhabha Atomic Research Center (BARC), set up in 1954, helped produce in-house more than half the initial fuel charge for the natural uranium heavy-water research reactor CIRUS, which went "critical" in 1960. The CIRUS enterprise was undertaken with Canadian cooperation. The American-supplied commercial light-water power reactor at Tarapur became operational in 1969. The United States supplied this, India's first power reactor, with fuel.[2] Until the Indian nuclear explosion in May 1974, there was a great deal of interaction between the growing number of experts in India and their Western counterparts, particularly Canadians. While there could have been many projects under joint Canadian-Indian leadership, the Indians wanted to develop their own centers for electronics and fuel cycle technologies.[3] The price for self-reliance was delay, making India susceptible to international pressure once the 1974 explosion had publicized its future weapons capability. By the end of the 1970s, India came under increasing pressure from the United States and Canada to accept full-scope safeguards and to sign the Nonproliferation Treaty (NPT). Only the Soviets did not insist on full-scope safeguards for the supply of heavy water.

The Indian explosion stimulated thinking in Pakistan about the questionable dependability of conventional arms supply and the independent nuclear option. Pakistan had the infrastructure for developing nuclear energy when, in 1956, it established the Atomic Energy Commission. Its first nuclear power plant was set up in 1965 with Canadian help. The first cadres of Pakistan's scientists were trained in the West, mostly in the United States. The U.S. arms cutoff in the midst of the 1965 Indo-Pakistan war and the loss of East Pakistan to India in 1971 left Pakistanis feeling vulnerable, which fostered thoughts of a stronger nuclear program. The political elite saw the nuclear option as the instrument of national salvation, by providing a reliable strategic deterrence against superior Indian conventional capability. National prestige was less weighty a factor in Pakistani thinking than in Indian. For Pakistan, the nuclear weapons option was more an act of desperation to build a weapon of "last resort."

Pakistan and France signed an agreement in March 1976 for the supply of a nuclear reprocessing plant. Whereas the 1965 Canadian deal to assist the Pakistani program did not elicit negative reactions from the United States, the French agreement came under immediate attack for two reasons. First, the Pakistani pursuit of a nuclear weapons option was clear by that time. Second, while the Canadian deal for the nuclear power plant was covered by a safeguards agreement with the IAEA that allowed for inspections to ensure that no nuclear materials were diverted for bombs, the French reprocessing plant did not provide for such safeguards. Thus, in American eyes, the deal signaled the serious possibility of a weapons capability. Consequently, the United States pressed for full-scope safeguards for Pakistan's existing research and power facilities. The United States did not subscribe to the theory that India's or Pakistan's acquisition of a weapons capability would make war unthinkable in South Asia. Rather, Washington feared that it would simply lead to conventional wars going nuclear. In order to dissuade Pakistan from taking the nuclear weapons path, and despite the special U.S.-Pakistan relationship, the Ford administration spent a great deal of energy trying to get France to cancel its nuclear deal. But by then a legal agreement was in place, and Zulfikar Ali Bhutto warned France that future military hardware sales would be contingent on its first fulfilling the contractual obligation on the reprocessing plant.

The United States sought to formulate an overall policy on the export of sensitive nuclear technology and to coordinate exports with other potential suppliers. But France's Framatome and Germany's Kraftwerke Union began to land lucrative contracts in the developing world and needed the export markets to support their domestic industries. Initially the Europeans resisted the efforts by Canada and the United States to undermine their deals. By 1976 nonproliferation had become an issue in the American presidential campaign, and Ford was under pressure to show an effort of good faith. Thus, Kissinger arrived in Pakistan in August 1976 with a tough message calling for the cancellation of the reprocessing plant deal. Although he offered A-7 aircraft, he was unable to convince Bhutto to make this exchange. While the military may have welcomed some help with the rapidly deteriorating conventional arms balance against India, no one was willing to give up the French deal for the possibility of future supply of aircraft from the United States.

The advent of the Carter administration elevated nonproliferation to the forefront of American foreign policy concerns, and South Asia came under immediate scrutiny. Because of suspicions that the Canadian-supplied CIRUS had been the progenitor of the 1974 nuclear device, the U.S. agreement for the supply of heavy water for the Tarapur plant ran into difficulty. India's large research and energy program was subject to review, and the United States called for full-scope safeguards as a precondition for any future cooperation. Furthermore, the earlier U.S.-Pakistan quarrel over the reprocessing plant became public.[4]

The United States put several restrictions in place under the Nuclear Nonproliferation Act of 1978 and prohibited the export of nuclear-related materials without full-scope IAEA safeguards. The London Suppliers Group coordinated the restrictions through a common policy. Under considerable American pressure, France announced a new nuclear export procedure in September 1976. After a visit to Washington the following month, the French president, Giscard d'Estaing, declared "discontinuation until further notice of the export of reprocessing facilities."[5]

The Symington and Glenn amendments to the Foreign Assistance Act of 1979 called for an end to all assistance to any country receiving enrichment or reprocessing technology.[6] Consequently, the Carter administration ended nuclear cooperation with India and Pakistan. In 1979 rumors stirred that assistance in nuclear development for economic and military purposes could be revived if full-scope safeguards went into effect, but neither India nor Pakistan was willing to accept these stipulations.

The chilly atmosphere in U.S.-Pakistan relations for much of the Carter presidency was not surprising given Carter's view that nuclear proliferation was one of the greatest dangers facing the international system and that the possession of nuclear technology made every conflict a potential nuclear one. Pakistan did not share this assessment, believing instead that the possession of the technology was not an issue since the problems of national security required Pakistan to pursue this option. Pakistan advocated the United States focus on the entire gamut of its security problems. It expected its longtime American friend to be understanding of its concerns. Nonetheless, the stalemate continued until the Soviet Union invaded Afghanistan.

CONTAINING PROLIFERATION

The Reagan administration found itself having to manage the twin problems of nuclear nonproliferation and the Afghanistan war. Senior Carter officials had held the view that Pakistan must understand and subscribe to U.S. goals limiting the nuclear club to its recognized members. Only then would there be a substantial package of assistance in the fight against the Soviets in Afghanistan. The discussions that followed the change of administrations were within the broad guidelines of finding an appropriate formula combining the above concerns.

In actuality, the political climate for U.S.-Pakistan talks had begun to change in the last months of the Carter administration. Deputy Secretary of State Warren Christopher conducted talks with Pakistani leaders in an attempt to find a way to help them understand and then combat the new challenge on Pakistan's northern border. While Zia rejected Christopher's offer of $400 million in assistance, calling it "peanuts," he did not fail to appreciate the newfound place for Pakistan in American foreign policy. Under these new conditions, the former acrimonious and accusatory tone of the dialogue was replaced by a genuine desire by both parties to find a way around the impasse.

A common strategy evolved quickly with the Reagan administration. James Buckley, undersecretary of state for political-military affairs, went to Islamabad in 1981 and received assurances from Zia that he would not embarrass the United States in the nuclear area. These assurances provided the basis for seeking and obtaining legislation from Congress authorizing a waiver of the Symington amendment for the duration of the five-year assistance program, without which the president would have had to certify that Pakistan had ceased all efforts to acquire a nuclear weapon.

Zia stated that to be meaningful, the U.S. security assistance package needed to be both substantial and long-term in order to defeat the Soviets in Afghanistan and end their threat to Pakistan and the Persian Gulf region. The United States accepted this point of view. In turn, Zia understood the condition that American law precluded aid without a specific presidential request for a waiver in the interest of U.S. national security. The president would not ask for such waivers unless Pakistan abided by the letter and the spirit of the law.

By the time Zia went to the United States on a state visit in December 1982, he showed how well he understood the rules of the renewed relationship. He asked for a demonstrable signal of the American commitment in the form of state-of-the-art technology. This was to be the F-16 interceptor aircraft, the sale of which could be defended on the basis of Pakistan's need to protect itself against the increasing border violations by Afghanistan. The request was neither simple nor a good litmus test of the U.S. commitment. First, the F-16 had certain proprietary technology that would never be sold to Pakistan. Consequently, modifications were necessary before the aircraft could be sold. Second, Congress would have to be convinced both of the Pakistani need and of the credibility of Zia's promise to curtail the nuclear program.

In addition to the sale of 40 F-16As, the security assistance package included new items for air defense, such as radar, surface-to-air and air-to-air missiles, artillery, artillery rounds, antitank missiles and radars for firepower enhancement, light helicopters for mobility, harpoon missiles, radar for the navy, and several hundred reconditioned M-48A5 medium tanks for the army. It was a substantial package, and the administration made a persuasive case for congressional approval. After a waiver of the Symington and Glenn amendments, the multiyear assistance program to Pakistan began in earnest in 1983.[7]

The challenge in Afghanistan required improved relations between India and Pakistan. The United States focused on ways to achieve this goal, recognizing Pakistan's inability to sustain a two-front war. The publicly acknowledged fear in Islamabad in August 1984 that India was about to launch an attack against the Pakistani nuclear facilities alarmed the United States,[8] which sought some forward movement on the nuclear front, given the clear Pakistani message that any Indian attack on the nuclear facilities meant war. A presidential mission led by Michael Armacost, the undersecretary of state for political affairs, and Donald Fortier, the deputy assistant to the president for national security affairs, traveled to India and Pakistan. As reported in India, the U.S. officials wanted the countries to consider "regional initiatives to avert nuclear competition in the subcontinent."[9] While such suggestions were unpopular, both countries did move about three months later with their agreement not to attack each other's nuclear facilities.

However, American hopes for India's and Pakistan's adherence to the Nonproliferation Treaty got nowhere. As Rajiv Gandhi reminded the West, Indian opposition to the treaty was even older than the Pakistani nuclear program. Gandhi took the standard Indian position that the Pakistani weapons program was the real issue, not the applicability of the NPT, and that the United States had to focus on restricting the weapons supply to Pakistan rather than pressuring India to sign the NPT. Raja Ramanna, who as head of the Atomic Energy Commission had overseen the Indian program, pointed out that India considered the NPT doctrine, designed to discriminate between nuclear weapons states and nonnuclear weapons states as "repulsive as apartheid."[10] Pakistan got itself off the hook by saying that it was willing to subscribe to the NPT if India did the same. However, the NPT was clearly a nonstarter for these South Asian countries, and both Gandhi and Zia met separately with Reagan in October 1985 to discuss the nuclear issue.

In a variety of public and private forums, Zia denied that Pakistan had violated any of its agreements with the United States and assured the Americans that no nuclear weapon existed. An era of intense dialogue between Zia and the United States on limiting Pakistan's nuclear ambitions ensued. All of the key political actors in Islamabad understood that to cross the nuclear weapons threshold meant the immediate termination of assistance. Perhaps more than others, Zia understood that Pakistan could not withstand the pressure from the Soviets without the relationship with the United States; therefore, he was willing to engage the United States in serious promises on a matter of importance to American policy. The United States felt that while expecting Pakistan to abandon its nuclear program was not realistic, Pakistani capability could be capped and Pakistani leaders could be relied on to keep their word.[11]

Indian leaders worried that Pakistan had already acquired the capability to make a nuclear bomb by the mid-1980s and cited American press reports of its imminent test, perhaps in China. Such reports reintroduced China to the nuclear debate in India and Pakistan, while China continued to be the preoccupation for India. China reminded all concerned that it had already stated that it would not be the first to use nuclear weapons (although that statement did not have a specific South Asian context). Reports of a follow-on agreement for continued U.S. assistance to Pakistan after 1987 were ill received in India, and during this period Gandhi focused his own meeting with Reagan on U.S.-Indian collaboration. Reagan assured Gandhi that the United States would oppose Pakistan's crossing the threshold of nuclear weapons and that Zia had promised to restrain the program.[12]

Zia, in his address to the special session of the United Nations marking its 40th anniversary, called for a regional approach to nonproliferation and asked that the subcontinent become a nuclear weapons–free zone. Gandhi's address reached beyond South Asia and called for a global crusade against hunger, racism, and nuclear weapons. He asked that comprehensive measures on a nondiscriminatory basis be implemented. The U.N. meetings were also a chance for Reagan to challenge the Soviets on a number of issues, including Afghanistan; and to gauge whether Soviet policy was in fact shifting away from a military solution in Afghanistan.[13]

Gandhi said publicly that Pakistan was "making—or has made—the bomb," basing his belief on its acquisition of a sufficient amount of enriched uranium.[14] Zia in turn complained that India already enjoyed "some nuclear devices for military use" of its own and that it was operating a newly operational plutonium-producing reactor without international safeguards.[15] Despite these criticisms, Gandhi and Zia were meeting each other in New York; this fact stirred favorable comment in the American media, since U.S. strategists viewed regional reconciliation as an essential element in preventing expansion of the "nuclear club." Indian and Pakistani delegations were aware that their respective leaders were the only ones from the Third World who met with Reagan—all others who did so were key American allies from the major industrialized democracies. The White House gave the non-Western appointments only to Gandhi and Zia as a signal of the "strong ties in South Asia."[16]

Gandhi's public rejection of the U.S. position that Pakistan did not have the bomb and his call for greater U.S. action against Pakistan did not negate his desire for a new U.S.-Indian relationship. The United States shared in this desire for stronger ties. It approved an Indian request for the GE-404 engine for the planned Indian light combat aircraft, a decision conveyed by the Armacost-Fortier presidential mission in September 1985. Subsequent to the release of the jet engine and prior to the New York meeting between Reagan and Gandhi, Indians commented that "the Reagan administration appears to be quite keen on improving relations with India in every possible way by responding to the friendly gestures of Mr. Rajiv Gandhi's government."[17] However, India remained unconvinced by U.S. assurances that Pakistan had not developed a nuclear capability, and Gandhi acknowledged that Reagan had urged him to come to some agreement with Zia on a real improvement in relations between India and Pakistan before "a point of no return" was reached.[18] In other words, India needed to help put a brake on the Pakistani program.

By the time of the second Gandhi visit to Washington, in October 1987, bilateral trade had expanded, collaboration between the private sectors had intensified, cooperation in defense production was on the upswing, and, following the implementation of the memorandum of understanding on technology transfer, the United States had been contracted to launch Indian satellites. A fund for cultural, scientific, and educational cooperation also had been inaugurated, and bilateral coordination against terrorism was under way. In his remarks on the occasion of the visit, President Reagan stated that powerful political, economic, and cultural currents were drawing the two countries together. Announcing eight new agreements, Reagan added that in his talks he had urged India and Pakistan to "intensify their dialogue to build greater mutual confidence, to resolve outstanding issues, and to deal with the threat of nuclear proliferation in the region."[19] In his response, Prime Minister

Gandhi spoke of the newly realized promise of bilateral relations, which he credited to President Reagan's "personal attention and interest." Pointing to India's stand against vertical and horizontal proliferation, Gandhi acknowledged that time "is not on our side." India, he said, did not have any nuclear weapons and had no intention of producing any "unless constrained to do so." Although Gandhi did not name Pakistan, he pointed to the fact that "another country now seems on the threshold of fulfilling a long-time goal of acquiring nuclear weapons."

Earlier in 1987, Zia had broken his long silence on the issue of nuclear weapons technology in an interview in which he said that there was little "difficulty with building a bomb" and that Pakistan had never said that it was "incapable" of doing so. Rather, Zia said, Pakistan did not have weapons-grade enriched uranium because it had given an assurance that it would not perform any nuclear experiments for military purposes. Zia promised that he would abide by this commitment. He believed that Congress would come through with assistance for his country because of the higher stakes involved with fighting the Soviets in Afghanistan rather than focusing on "Pakistan's tiddly-widdly nuclear program."[20]

Concern with the Pakistani capacity for enriching uranium to weapons grade and rumors of the country's continued attempts to acquire such uranium led to U.S. legislation warning it not to engage or even attempt to engage in illegal export of U.S. technology. Pakistan objected that, with the measures in place, it was not even able to obtain "screws." As Zia correctly reckoned, the dilemma was one that pitted the U.S. interest in the Soviet withdrawal from Afghanistan against its desire to be strict on nonproliferation. Zia understood that the best American alternative was for Pakistan to agree to contain its enrichment program along with encouraging a regional solution involving the cooperation of India and Pakistan.

All of the restrictive amendments in the United States provided for a presidential waiver determining that a cutoff in funding to Pakistan would be "seriously prejudicial" to American objectives to contain nuclear proliferation or otherwise impair "the common defense and security." In a letter to their colleagues, senior Senators Bill Bradley and John Glenn argued that a breakdown over the nuclear issue with Pakistan would have broad repercussions by involving the 130 countries that were signatories of the NPT. They noted that India might be forced to act if Pakistani policy did not change. Illegal Pakistani exports from the United States also undermined the efforts to curtail trade from other sources in dual-use technology. The senators concluded that the choice facing the United States was not between supplying Pakistan for the defense of Afghanistan or Pakistan's nuclear program, but rather whether the United States would exercise its responsibility to reduce the risk of nuclear war or not. They argued that all assistance to Pakistan must be predicated on a total halt of the production of weapons-grade nuclear materials. Despite his subsequent fame, Senator Larry Pressler's role in the exercise was almost accidental. He offered to introduce an administration amendment to substitute for a version put forward by Senator Alan Cranston that had already passed the Senate Foreign Relations Committee; Cranston's version would have imposed an impossible certification requirement for continuation of aid. The Pressler version was passed, which stated that there could be no assistance or military sales to Pakistan unless the president certified in writing to Congress in the year that assistance or sale was contemplated that "Pakistan does not possess a nuclear explosive device and that the proposed United States assistance program will reduce significantly the risk that Pakistan will possess a nuclear explosive device," was thus passed as the lesser of two evils.

After careful consideration and an annual exercise of American soul-searching, presidential waivers were granted annually to the Pakistani assistance package. The waiver for 1987 was accompanied by the unusual step of a public White House statement noting that it was based on the recognition that "disrupting one of the pillars of the U.S. relationship with Pakistan would be counterproductive to the strategic interests of the United States, destabilizing for South Asia, and unlikely to achieve the nonproliferation objectives sought by the sponsors [of the legislation]." The statement went on to note that despite the problems, Pakistan would exercise restraint in critical areas. Furthermore, there was to be no diminution of the U.S. interest in restraining the spread of nuclear weapons in the subcontinent.[21]

The timing of that debate on the Pakistani program—July 1987—coincided with the escalation of tensions in the Persian Gulf and the beginning of an American naval escort of Kuwaiti oil tankers. It was not the time for a showdown with Pakistan, particularly as it seemed that the Soviets finally were starting to realize that they could not win in Afghanistan. While a move in the Senate in mid-1987 to withhold $110 million out of the $625 million planned for the following year was avoided, there were serious discussions with Zia on the need to deliver on his promise of nuclear restraint and to stop any upgrading of the nuclear program. Zia insisted that the operation to smuggle technology from the United States was a rogue one without government sanction. Pakistan also continued to point to the "American double standard" in forgetting the Indian 1974 test and in overlooking the tensions in the Indo-Pakistan relationship. Nonetheless, Zia stated that he would keep his promise. Promises notwithstanding, the United States was said to have stepped up its monitoring of Pakistani procurement activities to ensure compliance with the tighter procedures that Pakistan said it had put in place.[22]

The interview by A.Q. Khan, the key Pakistani nuclear engineer, in late February 1987 on Pakistan's nuclear capability had an unsettling effect on American opinion. Khan told an Indian journalist that Pakistan was nuclear weapons–capable, a reality that had prevented an Indian attack in August 1984.[23] The interview seemed to be a not-so-subtle attempt by Zia to put India and the West on notice that the fundamental equation had changed. Despite growing fear of a drift toward the competitive acquisition of nuclear weapons in South Asia, Undersecretary Armacost publicly stated that the Reagan administration's characterization of the Pakistani program was unchanged.[24] India, dismayed, concluded that Pakistan had sent a signal to the United States that, henceforth, assistance had to be provided unconditionally if the Americans wanted to pursue their Afghan policy.[25]

As pressure mounted from the United States to open its facilities to inspection, Pakistan publicly began to stress that the war in Afghanistan had inflicted high costs. Refugees, drugs, and guns were the lasting legacy, and terrorism now was prevalent in several cities. The government held the Afghan intelligence apparatus responsible in its attempts to weaken support for the war inside Pakistan. Zia pointed to the many sacrifices his country had made for the joint effort against the Soviets. As Soviet and Afghan air violations were becoming more frequent and menacing, Pakistan asked the United States for radar surveillance aircraft. While the administration was sympathetic, it recognized that such aircraft would represent a major upgrading of the Pakistani capability, with ramifications for the Indo-Pakistan front.

The administration briefed Congress concerning the possibility of granting an airborne early warning (AEW) capability to Pakistan. Edward Gnehm, a senior defense department official, publicly testified to the 400 violations of Pakistani airspace by the Soviets. He said that previous attempts to upgrade Pakistan's capability with the use of ground-based radar and the addition of Stingers and AIM-9L air-to-air missiles had been inadequate. The administration was sensitive to the fact that the Soviet Union was testing the new civilian government of Prime Minister Mohammed Khan Junejo. As American AEW assets were limited, Washington considered arranging their loan from a third country. In the meantime, interim measures were needed. Throughout the discussion of AEW, the United States declared that in helping on the Afghan front, it would "not create new tensions or misunderstandings with India since the advice and the assistance we are providing to Pakistan, including discussion of providing AEW capability is not directed at India."[26] The Asian and Pacific Affairs subcommittee chairman, Stephen Solarz, spoke for many when he responded that it was important that the United States help Pakistan in the circumstances but that care had to be exercised that the U.S.-Indian relationship was not harmed or Indo-Pakistani relations destabilized.

Indian unhappiness mounted with the Pakistani request for the purchase of AEW capability to fly continuous air patrols in conjunction with its F-16s. Such a capability could enable Pakistan to look deep into Indian territory and to provide cover for any proposed attack. Experts expected the provision of the E-2C to Pakistan to require 150 U.S. ground personnel; if the E-3A were provided, that number would rise to 200.[27] Neither Pakistan nor the United States was enthusiastic on that score. The sale or lease of the advanced E-3A was made more difficult because of the U.S.

deployment in the Persian Gulf at that time. Yet the United States wanted to comply with the request, since the war in Afghanistan was changing course and continued pressure on the Soviets was important.

The five-year assistance program expired on September 30, 1987, and was to be followed by a six-year program. This coincided with a case against a Canadian national of Pakistani origin, Arshad Pervez, who was caught trying to smuggle nuclear-related material out of the United States. Although Pakistan denied that any of its officials or agencies were involved, American pressure increased to cut off aid assistance just when the proposed new package came under scrutiny. More important for the future of U.S. relations with Pakistan, the credibility of Pakistani leaders suffered further as American officials and members of Congress recalled the many pledges they had been given that Pakistan was not engaged in a nuclear weapons program when in fact just the opposite appeared to be the case. A second difficulty was the identification of the Pakistani effort as representing support for the "Islamic bomb." To the United States and its allies, this gave Pakistan's program an even more sinister hue. A third complicating factor was A.Q. Khan's boast about Pakistan's nuclear capability.[28] Pakistan's China connection was also seen by Washington as a means of speeding up the process through access to a "proven" design.[29]

All this created serious questions regarding the appropriateness of the assistance program. To overlook Pakistani behavior had repercussions for the 130 members of the NPT, who were watching closely. Senator Glenn urged putting the Pakistan assistance program on hold for one year; the new assistance package would start in 1988, the amount of military assistance would be limited (which would preclude any consideration of the more sophisticated airborne surveillance AWACS), and the proposed six-year program would be reduced to two years. In exchange, the senator offered a six-year waiver of the Symington and Glenn amendments to allow assistance to Pakistan subject to presidential certification that the nation did not possess a nuclear weapon and that U.S. assistance helped prevent it from gaining possession of nuclear weapons. Glenn further proposed an annual requirement for presidential certification: that the U.S. president receive reliable assurances that

Pakistan had ceased producing weapons-grade nuclear material. Reliable assurances meant "formal written commitments by Pakistan's political leadership, verified by on-site inspections of relevant facilities by designated representatives of the United States or by any other means the U.S. finds acceptable."[30] In the end, the Pervez case necessitated another presidential waiver, the Solarz amendment, which dealt with prohibited illegal exports from the United States. By July 1987, when the debate regarding the Pakistan nuclear program was under way, everyone in Congress was aware that the Afghan Mujahidin had begun to do well against the Soviets. In the end, there was little desire to penalize Pakistan just when heavy casualties were being inflicted on the Soviets, who were seriously considering withdrawal.[31]

For its part, Pakistan continued to press for a nondiscriminatory application of nonproliferation criteria. Zia had already made proposals in the regional context, namely that Pakistan would agree to either mutual or IAEA inspections, sign the NPT, and declare South Asia a nuclear weapons–free zone. India, on the other hand, felt that the Pakistani program had advanced despite its assurances to the contrary. India also felt that equal treatment of it and Pakistan on nuclear matters was unfair as it had voluntarily given up the weapons option after its only nuclear test more than two decades earlier.

Pakistan's posture of deliberate ambiguity offered it the option of keeping American assistance while signaling that Islamabad could deter any Indian action. The scare from the Indian military exercise Brass Tacks in 1986–87 fed the paranoia of those who supported keeping the nuclear option open on both sides of the Indo-Pakistan border. But the same ambiguity had consequences for support for the post-1987 assistance program. An increasing number of voices in Congress asked for additional measures to dissuade Pakistan from going further with its nuclear weapons program.

Pakistan's public statements continued to emphasize the country's willingness to consider any proliferation concerns in the regional context. Islamabad asserted that "Pakistan does not possess nor [does it] intend to possess nuclear weapons."[32] Supposedly this stand was the result of enlightened self-interest and not due to any outside pressure.

By the middle of 1987, the United States was already India's largest trading partner, and cooperation in science and technology was on the increase. The Indo-U.S. Presidential Science and Technology Initiative (STI) of 1987 signaled a strong commitment to a variety of areas, including health (immunology), agriculture, meteorology, oceanography, and material sciences. The STI sought to maximize funding and reduce paperwork so that projects could be evaluated quickly. After the signing of the memorandum of understanding on technology transfers, the number of items approved by the United States went up sharply, with roughly 50 percent of the bilateral trade in dollar amounts going for high-technology items. The new relationship was reflected in remarks by Frank C. Carlucci, national security advisor to the president, at a meeting of the India-U.S. Business Leaders Council (the first time that such a meeting was attended at that level of the American government), indicating that the United States wished to reinforce the growing ties with India. These ties would encompass research establishments, scientists and engineers, as well as the private sector, and be reflected in greater cultural contact and an increase in tourism.[33] The statement was received favorably in India, where it was duly noted that the United States had said it would help move India into the 21st century and go further in defense and space-based communications cooperation. Such an effort made particular sense at a time when India was moving toward economic deregulation.

The increased ties were expected to be of mutual benefit: India would become technologically advanced; the United States would gain commercially through sales of goods and technology. A strong and independent India, presumably with reduced ties to the Soviet Union, was clearly in the U.S. interest.

Longtime congressional concern with the nuclear programs of India and Pakistan crystallized into an unusual effort to address both programs in April 1987. The catalyst for the action was the publicity about Pakistan's program and focus on the new assistance program for that country. Unwilling to stop assistance, given the Afghan war, the next best option seemed to be an effort to try for a regional solution. Senator Robert Byrd offered an amendment to section 516 on "restrictions on assistance to Pakistan" that made assistance to Pakistan and the sale of the supercomputer to

India contingent on the start of a nuclear dialogue between the two countries within 60 days of the passage of the legislation. In a point that was designed to reassure India, the Byrd amendment sought to proscribe any modification of aircraft for the delivery of nuclear weapons. The amendment to section 516 sought reassurances from India that no plutonium separated from the spent fuel would be used in nuclear weapons. In return for this, the administration could consider the sale of an airborne electronic warfare system to India (although India did not seem interested in the sale). The proposal made India unhappy, as it equated its nuclear program with that of Pakistan. Delhi once again objected that there had been no weapons activity on its part, whereas it believed the Pakistanis were moving ahead in violation of the stated promises of restraint.

From the administration's point of view, the congressional proposal was the worst of all options, since it was likely to have a negative impact on nonproliferation goals by speeding up the nuclear programs, destroying the Afghan policy, which required Pakistani cooperation, and annoying both India and Pakistan. India worked hard to defeat the attempt, with Gandhi complaining that the amendment would impose impossible conditions on the transfer of technology to India.[34] Indian scientific leaders asserted once again that the equation of the nuclear programs of India and Pakistan was totally unacceptable.[35] What was also troubling was Washington's implied threat of U.S. opposition to loans from various multilateral lending institutions, such as the World Bank, the International Monetary Fund, and the Asian Development Bank. India laid some of the blame at the administration's door for agreeing that there was a regional component to the Pakistani nuclear issue even though senior American officials always stated that the bilateral aspect was key. The Byrd amendment was the only attempt aimed at both India and Pakistan, and it failed. A six-year waiver of the Symington and Glenn amendments was not approved; the administration settled for two years.

Even as Gandhi expressed unhappiness with the direction of the congressional debate over the subcontinent, he was quick to congratulate the United States and the Soviet Union for the agreement to eliminate medium-range land-based nuclear missiles from Europe. Hailing the December 1987 Washington summit as a success, he recalled that India had raised its voice against arms proliferation for the past 40 years. The event, the first agreement of its kind, was of historic significance. The agreement showed that, given political will, technical problems such as verification can be overcome. India's own goal remained the complete global elimination of nuclear weapons, as pointed out in the Delhi declaration.[36]

The year 1987 proved to be a watershed. The Afghan war turned decisively against the Soviet Union, Gorbachev expressed a readiness to consider withdrawal, Pakistan's nuclear program came under extended negative scrutiny, new waivers of U.S. law had to be won in order to start the second multiyear program of assistance for Pakistan, and technology transfers to India accelerated, with the United States replacing the United Kingdom and Germany as the leading exporter within one year.[37] That year also saw serious deterioration in the Indo-Pakistan relationship, subsequent to the Brass Tacks military exercises. President Reagan also had a second set of meetings with the leaders of both India and Pakistan and told them that tensions in the region needed to be lowered and a nuclear dialogue between the two must occur even as the United States urged restraints on Pakistan. Reagan pointed to the growing U.S.-Soviet arms control efforts as a model for future steps eliminating the threat of nuclear war. Despite American encouragement, India and Pakistan continued to resist signing the NPT. Pakistan said it would do so only if India signed. India said it could not for two reasons: first, the NPT was inherently discriminatory in favor of those who possessed nuclear weapons; and second, subscribers to the treaty violated it through tests and explosions.[38]

The first year of the six-year package for Pakistan was approved in December 1987. The $4.02 billion deal allotted 57 percent for economic assistance and 43 percent for concessional foreign military sales credits. Zia had insisted on keeping the economic portion higher than the military component. Pakistan would receive $638 million annually. The United States did not rule out supplying AEW capability if there was no change in Soviet policy. This was intended to both reassure Pakistan and create a substantial Indian stake in the withdrawal of Soviet forces from Afghanistan. In moving forward with the assistance package, the administration acknowledged its serious concern over the direction of the Pakistani nuclear program. Pakistani leaders were reminded once again of the "strength of the U.S. commitment to nonproliferation, as well as the depth of concern felt on this issue in Congress."[39] With the passage of the bill for 1988, the administration undertook further efforts to prevent a nuclear race in South Asia while acknowledging that nuclear weapons remained a popular option there and any government seen as compromising its sovereignty by unilaterally abandoning the nuclear option was not likely to survive.

Indian unhappiness with the U.S. assistance to Pakistan was summed up in an editorial that lamented Indian leaders' lack of realism in their belief that with the end of the Afghan crisis, American priorities had changed.[40] What this argument failed to acknowledge was that U.S. policy had been founded on the need to balance the U.S. relationship with Pakistan with a desire for real improvement with India. Furthermore, as long as the Soviets continued to stay in Afghanistan, the United States would not end support for Pakistan.

By early 1988, nuclear issues receded from the headlines as the Soviets prepared to withdraw from Afghanistan, and India and Pakistan seemed settled into a posture described by one expert as "non-weaponized deterrence."[41] The Geneva Accords were signed in April, and Soviet withdrawal began within 30 days. But the annual requirement for presidential certification based on the Pressler amendment meant that—sooner rather than later—the United States would focus on the nuclear issue as it tried to reconcile its own nonproliferation goals with the needs of the Afghan situation. That concern had been highlighted during the Iran-Iraq War by Iran's use of its Chinese-supplied Silkworm missiles. The prospective marriage of nuclear weapons capability with missiles meant that in the future, India and Pakistan could rapidly escalate the level of warfare.

Even before Soviet withdrawal was completed, President Zia died in a plane crash along with several other senior officers of the army and the American ambassador, Arnold Raphel. Zia had been a close ally in the Afghan war, and Raphel, a gifted senior member of the American Foreign Service, was a knowledgeable and respected individual known for his commitment to U.S.-Pakistan relations. As Secretary of State George Shultz left Washington to head the American delegation to Zia's funeral, the new government policy was far from clear. Ghulam Ishaq Khan, the incoming president, was a longtime bureaucrat with a reputation for inflexibility. As it turned out, he was to preside over the end of the special relationship between the United States and Pakistan.

ASSESSING PROLIFERATION UNDER CRISIS CONDITIONS

With the start of the Bush administration, U.S. policy toward South Asia was formulated in the context of the nearly completed Soviet withdrawal from Afghanistan. Vice President Bush had been active in the region. He had traveled there in 1984 and vividly remembered the visit and the subsequent contacts he had in Washington with Zia and Rajiv Gandhi. Gandhi had made a favorable impression on Bush when they first met at Mrs. Gandhi's residence in Delhi in May 1984. Her assassination and Rajiv Gandhi's accession to office touched Bush. By the time Gandhi came to the United States in 1985, he had already been elected in a massive vote of confidence, which added to his stature. Gandhi's desire for better relations with the United States and his willingness to open India to economic reform made him an attractive leader. Bush had hosted the Gandhis in Houston in 1985 and proudly shown Rajiv around its aerospace facilities, in deference to his former career as a pilot with a penchant for technology. On the other hand, Bush was disappointed with Zia. As a man with a strong personal code of conduct, Bush believed that when a gentleman gave his word, he kept it. He held Zia, a military officer, to his explicit promise that Pakistan did not possess and would not build a nuclear weapon.

Bush congratulated Benazir Bhutto after her electoral victory in 1988 and wished her success in the formation of a new government. He stressed the importance of elections in the democratic process and the need to abide by their results. The Pakistani military and its president clearly understood that message, as it paved Bhutto's way to the premiership.

George Bush had first broached the subject of Indo-Pakistan confidence-building measures in the course of his 1984 visit to the subcontinent. He hoped for a real breakthrough in relations between India and Pakistan, which would bring a brighter future to the entire region. Throughout his tenure as vice president, he had encouraged a dialogue between the two countries and had helped within the administration as needed. Therefore, when he became president, regional leaders expected that he would continue to be intimately involved.

Despite Bush's interest in foreign policy, however, domestic pressures and the opportunities created by the end of the Cold War competed for his time. Besides American preoccupations, a new set of Indian and Pakistani leaders themselves were not inclined to improve relations, nor were they as practical on the subject as Zia and Rajiv Gandhi had been. Ghulam Ishaq's anti-Indian predilections prevented any form of dialogue. He encouraged the bureaucracy and the scientific/military complex in its pursuit of anti-American and anti-Indian positions. Taken in combination, these factors had a harmful effect on U.S. relations with Pakistan.

By 1989, events inside Kashmir rekindled the possibility of war between India and Pakistan. Difficulties mounted after the ouster of Farooq Abdullah's elected government in Kashmir in July 1984. Gandhi was accused of having rigged the election, forcing collaboration between the Congress Party in Kashmir and the National Conference. Some of the Muslim United Front's younger cadre were among the first casualties in the mounting anti-Indian challenge. The problems escalated in late 1989, and by early 1990 a major popular outburst had begun. Delhi dispatched a new governor to the state along with a 150,000-member paramilitary force from the border security service.

At about the same time, Pakistan focused on Kashmir again. The earlier days of caution had died with Zia, and the genuinely difficult situation inside Indian Kashmir tempted Pakistan's leaders to raise the ante. Their political rhetoric increased along with the Kashmir uprising. They looked at the massive Kashmiri protest and willingness to fight Indian injustice as similar to the Mujahidin's successful war against the Soviet Union in Afghanistan. They decided to replicate, albeit on a much smaller scale, that indirect but well-organized support for the indigenous uprising. India accused Pakistan of using Pakistani and Afghan political groups and volunteers to provide arms and training and of encouraging a higher level of Islamic motivation. Benazir Bhutto, in her first term as prime minister, had accused the Indian government of "indulging in genocide" in Kashmir. Responding to that statement, the Indian prime minister, V.P. Singh, charged Pakistan with a "deep conspiracy" from across the border in Kashmir. Bhutto and Singh were both too weak to keep the issue from causing a general deterioration in relations between the countries.

For the United States, the mix of Kashmir and the real potential for nuclear war in the subcontinent was unnerving. Memories of Brass Tacks lingered along with the possibility of accidental war through miscalculation. The United States in March and April 1990 approached Russia, China, Japan, and key European Community governments to emulate its own demarches in both Delhi and Islamabad, urging a reduction in tension before unwanted escalation could take place. Some easing seemed to begin. However, the United States took no chances. Recognizing that presidential missions had signaled interest and urgency to India and Pakistan, the White House launched another one in May 1990 led by Robert Gates, the deputy national security advisor. As Gates explained, the danger of a nuclear confrontation between India and Pakistan loomed large and his mission was to lessen the chances for such an outcome.[42]

As tensions mounted, Bhutto left on a visit to key Muslim states looking for support on Kashmir. Her advisors continued to stress that the situation was deteriorating, despite the fact that Pakistan did not want war. When Gates arrived in Islamabad on May 20, 1990, Bhutto was still out of the country. In his meetings with the other main actors—the president and the chief of the army—Gates gave a sobering account of the situation in Kashmir and the difficulties inherent in the Pakistani stand. According to the public account given by the American ambassador present at the meeting, Gates told the Pakistan leadership that if they were to start a war with India, they could not count on any help from the United States. He reportedly added that the United States was not saying that Pakistan was initiating the conflict as such. However, "perhaps by supporting the Kashmiris in a way analogous to the Mujahidin in Afghanistan, it could make a basic change in the equation between Pakistan and India."[43]

In New Delhi, the Indian prime minister told Gates that an end of Pakistan's support for terrorism in Kashmir and the Punjab was the prerequisite for any dialogue with that country. Gates asked both sides to end their military confrontation and work out their differences through negotiations. Washington was not willing to lose nearly a decade of efforts spent building better U.S. bilateral relations with both countries and using that improvement to build bridges between them. While the United States did not offer itself as a potential mediator, it did offer some ideas for confidence-building measures in the subcontinent. By June 1990, there was a clear relaxation on both sides, bilateral talks took place, and an agreement was reached on several confidence-building measures.

Shortly after the Gates mission, in October 1990, the United States terminated its assistance to Pakistan since the president was no longer able to certify to Congress that the country did not have a nuclear weapon. The United States continued to demand transparency in the Pakistani nuclear program as the price of assistance. Two years later, in the course of Deputy Secretary of State Strobe Talbot's visit to Pakistan in September 1994, the Clinton administration also tried to get Pakistan to agree to inspections, if not a rollback of the program. Pakistan stuck to its position that nothing could be done unless India also accepted the measures.[44] Pakistan and China also disputed the charge that China had supplied the M-11 missile to Pakistan and called the American threat of sanctions unfair, claiming it was based on faulty information. India found cold comfort in China's denial, for those missiles could take Pakistan's military to the next level of capability. Islamabad pointed to India's own development of the Agni and the Prithvi missiles. The United States let all parties know that the 1987 missile technology control regime (MTCR) guidelines were sacrosanct and no violation was to be tolerated. Pakistani leaders continued to point out that the American efforts aimed at nonproliferation were one-sided against Pakistan and failed to address the Indo-Pakistan context of the policy. They highlighted their "responsible" behavior in not exploding a device, in not transferring it to another state, in not acting in a provocative manner internationally, in holding the line against drugs and terrorism, and in participating in peacekeeping operations within the U.N. context.[45]

After the assistance cutoff to Pakistan in 1990, the United States briefly tried to engage India and Pakistan in regional talks to discuss ways of dealing with their nuclear programs and security concerns. India remained opposed to signing the NPT, and Pakistan continued to say that it would do so only if India did. Meanwhile the NPT came under reconsideration in 1995, and the United States mounted a major international effort for its permanent extension. There was little to suggest that India would change its stance on the discriminatory nature of the NPT. Calling the 1995 permanent extension of the treaty "the legitimisation for the foreseeable future and beyond, of the possession of nuclear weapons by a few states and their possible use as a currency of power," the Indian delegate to the Geneva talks reminded the world that nonproliferation in the absence of disarmament was unacceptable and called for a phased program with the eventual aim of elimination of all nuclear weapons within a time-bound framework.[46] Prime Minister Rao criticized the NPT extension as a perpetuation of the efforts of a few to maintain their monopoly over the means of mutual destruction. He supported the aims of the next steps in the process, namely, the Comprehensive Test Ban Treaty (CTBT) and the Convention for the Cut-off of Fissile Materials, but urged that attention be turned to the achievement of universal and comprehensive nuclear disarmament.[47] Indians pointed to their long-standing support for global disarmament and to the Rajiv Gandhi Action Plan, unveiled in 1988, which had mapped out a program for the elimination of all nuclear weapons by the year 2000. Clearly that timetable had slipped, but Indian negotiators in Geneva working on the CTBT held fast on the issue of a time-bound schedule for global nuclear disarmament.

While expressing reservations regarding some components of the CTBT draft, such as on-site inspections and the scope of the treaty, Pakistan pledged its support. Islamabad seemingly reckoned that Indian hesitation would play in its favor and that the CTBT would preclude further Indian testing, which would, if carried out: (1) refine and upgrade the Indian nuclear weapons capability, and (2) cause nuclear hawks in Pakistan to press to match the test, thereby rekindling the fires of a nuclear weapons race that Pakistan was sure to lose. Pakistan expressed itself officially as being in favor of an early conclusion of the treaty prohibiting the production of fissile material despite the fact that the treaty would perpetuate the asymmetry in India's and Pakistan's stockpiles. According to the Pakistani statement, "our concern about the asymmetry in stockpiles between India and Pakistan can be effectively addressed in a variety of ways."[48]

The U.S. position was articulated by John Holum, the director of the Arms Control and Disarmament Agency (ACDA). Reminding the Conference on Disarmament that the United Nations had pledged that the CTBT would be signed in 1996, he urged that the work be completed prior to the June deadline so that the treaty could be presented to the General Assembly for signature in September of that year. He argued that the CTBT went a long way toward the Indian goal of complete disarmament as it is "a profoundly important new constraint, *especially* on the nuclear weapon states." Second, he stated that the CTBT is an "indispensable step if the ultimate elimination of nuclear arms is ever to be achieved."[49] Holum acknowledged that the CTBT would fundamentally constrain the advancement of a nuclear weapons capability rather than simply its acquisition. Thus it seemed to run into Indian opposition, as it lacked the fixed time-bound framework for elimination of all nuclear weapons.

Following Benazir Bhutto's April 1995 visit to Washington, the Clinton administration took a fresh look at the Pressler amendment in an attempt to find ways to cooperate with Pakistan in areas where it was in the American interest to do so.[50] No lifting of the ban on military sales and assistance was contemplated, but Clinton promised Bhutto that Washington would try to find a way to deal with U.S. unfairness in keeping both the F-16s Pakistan had already paid for as well as the money paid. In May 1995, the House adopted a provision to retain the ban on arms assistance but allowed economic and humanitarian assistance dealing with antinarcotics, international military education and training (IMET), antiterrorism, aviation safety, immigration, peacekeeping activities, and the promotion of U.S. trade and investment. This amendment also supported the sale of the embargoed F-16s to a third party and the reimbursement to Pakistan from the proceeds of the sale, plus the release of equipment Pakistan had sent to the United States for repairs, so long as the repairs or upgrading had not been carried out.

In May 1995, the Senate Foreign Relations Committee approved (by a vote of 16 to 2) a similar amendment to Section 620E of the Foreign Assistance Act of 1961. Known as the Brown amendment, it modified the Pressler restrictions and, while keeping the military ban in place, allowed the flow of economic and humanitarian assistance to Pakistan along with help on the antinarcotics front, for IMET, and for antiterrorism and peacekeeping activities. The amendment, ratified by the full Senate in September, also allowed the administration to release Pakistan from its obligations to pay for the storage of the 28 undelivered F-16s contracted for by Pakistan with a payment of $658 million and the return of unrepaired military equipment to Pakistan, but kept the MTCR sanctions in place. It also called for an administration report on steps toward regional nonproliferation objectives. After resolution in conference and legislative hurdles involving the overall bill to which it was attached, the Brown amendment finally cleared Congress in late January and was signed in to law by the president on January 26, 1996.

In sum, the nuclear issue complicated the U.S. relationship with Pakistan and generally lowered the level of American political and strategic dialogue with the subcontinent. Many aspects of the carefully nurtured relationship built over the years with India and, in particular, with Pakistan were allowed to atrophy. That the breakdown occurred under the leadership of President Bush was indeed unfortunate, as he had been central to the improvement of American ties with both countries and with U.S. attempts to push for Indo-Pakistan normalization. With the termination of the U.S.-Pakistan relationship, Indo-Pakistani relations took a turn for the worse. The careful U.S. nurturing of a rapprochement in the subcontinent did not survive the uprising in Kashmir; just when it was important to keep the dialogue open, the downturn in relations ended the search for a way out of the Kashmir and nuclear problems. After 1990, a distracted Washington focused on events elsewhere but concern about nuclear weapons and a desire to move forward on the NPT, the CTBT, and the Fissile Material Cut-off discussions forced reengagement with India and Pakistan on nuclear matters. In the meantime, the United States made few attempts to work toward a bilateral agenda with Pakistan even as the administration moved forward on modifying the Pressler legislation. Neither was there any movement on regional nuclear discussions once India insisted on enlarging the participants to include not just the nuclear and near-nuclear powers but others such as Iraq, Iran, and Saudi Arabia. Various gains made in past years were lost because of Washington's lack of sustained interest, particularly within the senior ranks of the government, and the absence of the Soviet Union from the picture. As the United States celebrated the end of the Cold War, it needed a new focus to reengage in the subcontinent. The economic relationship among the United States, India, and Pakistan would provide some of that focus.

4

The Economic Imperatives

CONVENTIONAL WISDOM HAS IT THAT FUTURE ECOnomic relations will dictate the overall nature of U.S. relationships with India and Pakistan. That assumption is based on the expectation that these South Asian countries will continue to integrate themselves into the world economy and take part actively in trade and investment with the United States. Both have adopted economic liberalization policies aimed at attracting foreign investment in response to the American search for markets. Once such investments are made, it is assumed that the United States will have a clearer stake in the future of India and Pakistan.

This chapter concentrates on four issues of direct interest to the United States: the question of public versus private sectors in the future; the staying power of economic reforms and their likely pace of implementation; access of American goods to Indian and Pakistani markets; and the attractiveness of each country for American investment.

RIDING THE TIGER

Political leaders in the subcontinent have been extremely wary of undertaking fundamental shifts in the economic policies of their countries. The one main exception in Pakistan was the 1970 election platform of the Pakistan's People's Party (PPP) under which Z.A. Bhutto pledged to nationalize some of the largest companies (steel, fertilizer, engineering, banking, etc.) in order to break the monopoly of the "22 families" who had been the driving force behind and principal beneficiaries of the nation's economic development in the 1960s. Bhutto's attempt at creating a large public sector overnight had a disastrous effect on investment and destroyed the very industries that he had hoped to make showpieces.

The debate on the appropriate balance between the public and private sectors has always been of interest to the United States. During the 1950s, when key decisions on the subject were made in India, Washington noted that the advocates for the public sector were the same ones who espoused closer links with Moscow during the Cold War.[1]

The "public sector" in India, therefore, was regarded negatively in the United States, which resented the fact that the Soviet Union was involved with its establishment. Over the years, many Americans pointed to the Indian public sector and its performance as indicative of everything that was wrong with Soviet economic policy. Americans asserted that the private sector was an important companion effort at spreading the advantages of economic development, involving millions of people who otherwise might well have been left out of the mainstream.

Public-sector inefficiency was masked by the special terms of barter that the Soviet Union had set up with India, through which the Soviets committed themselves to buy Indian manufactured products. The Indian government was another customer for the goods produced in the large public sector. In fact, 10 to 15 percent of its output was slated for compulsory purchase by government departments. Output from the public-sector steel mills was used by the railways, among others. Steel produced at the massive Soviet-built plants was bartered with the Soviets for other goods. Thus, India did not have to compete in the open market to sell items produced by its public sector, which also served the function of employing and training a large portion of the national labor force.

Public-sector problems sharpened as the plants aged and required major investments to upgrade. By that time, the Soviets were less inclined or able to become heavily involved in India, and the war in Afghanistan had dulled the attraction of the Soviet model for India. With the weakened Soviet hold on the countries of Eastern Europe, India found itself becoming less competitive there. Moreover, the opening of Eastern Europe to the West and to Japan in the late 1980s made it harder for India to make the necessary economic deals. But of course, the harshest shock to the Indian public sector came with the demise of the Soviet Union and the loss of the republics where India had special agreements.

Extensive soul-searching took place in India subsequent to the Soviet political collapse. The discrediting of the public sector within Russia obviously made it tougher for a country like India where, for local reasons, the model was already tarnished. The debate in Delhi sharpened with the decision of the Rao government to introduce a new economic policy.

Wanting a clear break with past trends, the Rao government initiated twofold reforms in 1991 aimed at: (1) redefining the relative roles of the public and private sectors in the economy, and (2) integrating India into the international economy.[2] As articulated by the Indian government, the reform process was to be far-reaching and sustained. The general objective was to reduce poverty. Both goals required a sustained effort to maintain the momentum of the broad-based reform effort, support for and from the private sector, and a reduction of state involvement in the financial, social, and infrastructure sectors.

The U.S. reaction was highly positive. Washington assessed the reforms as bold and broad in scope. Today, several years later, some policies, such as those for external deregulation, are being reformed more rapidly than others. Areas that received the least attention are structural measures to reduce the fiscal deficit and public enterprise and labor market policies. Despite the uneven nature of the follow-up, the comprehensivness and pace of reform generated credibility for the process. However, the pace and, to some extent, the prioritization of reforms caused delays in investment decisions.

Two views on the sequencing of Indian reforms exist. The first is the commonly held belief that sequencing should be dictated by the economic logic, beginning with price deregulation and trade policy reform while reducing the fiscal deficit and following with more institution-sensitive reforms, such as those for public enterprises and labor. The second recognizes that in order to be successful, reform must build "an alliance between the gainers from the reform to offset the pressures from the losers," often implying undertaking the easier steps first.[3] Despite the persistence of the fiscal deficit, the Indian program has done well in balancing the pressures and in following logical economic policies. Yet the measures adopted thus far have been the relatively easy ones. The tougher structural reforms are yet to come.

The welfare of India's dynamic private sector is of great interest to the United States, whose own private sector has generally reacted favorably to the reforms. The foreign private sector has been more enthusiastic than has been its Indian domestic counterpart. The reforms thus far have increased foreign private capital flows and stimulated the imagination of American investors. Indians point out that their country has a strong entrepreneurial class and a complementary "rule of law" system for its support.

ASSESSING REFORMS

The 1991 package provided the following incentives for private-sector investment:

- The elimination of import licensing requirements and lower tariffs for capital and intermediate goods
- Trade account convertibility of the rupee
- Removal of the requirement for government approval of domestic investment applications except for a negative list of 15 industries defined as sensitive
- A partial opening of the infrastructure and financial structures through a reduction in the number of areas reserved exclusively for the public sector (from 18 to 6)
- Automatic approval by the Reserve Bank of India of new foreign investments that involve up to 51 percent equity participation in local ventures
- Liberalization of capital markets, including opening them up to foreign institutional investors, and creating an independent authority to regulate them

The prospect of India becoming a dynamic emerging market generated great excitement in the United States. Portfolio investment demonstrated the pull as it increased from $200 million in 1991 to $3 billion for 1993–94. Indians were disappointed, however, at the slow rate of foreign direct investment and in the cautious rate of joint venture agreements; they contrasted this with the speed with which American business invested in China, despite greater apparent difficulties.

The difficulties confronting the private sector have caused the slower than expected investment. These difficulties include higher corporate taxes than those in other countries undertaking reform (at a level between 50 and 65 percent based on the category of the firm), the continuing ban on consumer goods, and the fact that many tariffs are still high when compared with those of other countries (10 to 15 percent in most reforming Latin American economies and 35 percent in East Asian ones). Other factors are an overburdened judicial system that does not provide a timely resolution of commercial and regulatory disputes and an unpredictable regulatory body despite the reforms, particularly in the areas of labor, land, and capital markets. For those without access to domestic or foreign capital markets, the inefficiencies of the financial system remain a problem. The major infrastructure deficiencies are another hindrance since, for example, there is still a power shortfall of 19 percent at peak times. Telecommunications problems exist as well; India has the lowest telephone density ratio in Asia. Roads and railways are in poor shape, and the ports are below international standards and have a history of difficult labor relations.

Yet, the Indian domestic private sector has been revitalized. After a sharp decline in 1991–92, exports were up by 20 percent in 1992–93 and a further 18 percent in 1994–95. The greatest gains were in the technology-intensive and labor-intensive areas, such as the software, garment, and leather industries. The matching of Indian goods with foreign technology and marketing is expected to provide handsome dividends for domestic enterprises and their foreign partners.

With the increase in portfolio investment comes the opportunity of access to nondebt foreign savings and integration into the international economy. Of course, the positive impact of reserves on India should permit a faster pace of tariff liberalization. However, portfolio capital flows can be unpredictable and volatile, and access to international markets has implications for domestic economic policies. Such flows can affect the exchange rate and cause a decline in export growth.

The underlying model for India's economic reforms appears to be China's "shrinking approach," whereby the public sector stagnates and shrinks in size relative to the growing private sector. Fiscal adjustment becomes a key element of the approach, both to reduce inflation and help coordinate the private sector.

In the context of fiscal adjustment, India sees the value-added tax as the one tax measure that could raise as much as 2 percent of the gross domestic product (GDP) in revenue. Despite the 1991 reforms India has been facing a continuing deficit (8.5 percent of GDP in 1990–91, 6.5 percent in 1991–92, 5.7 percent in 1992–93—divided at 2 percent for the states, 1 percent for public enterprises, and 3 percent for the federal government). The deficit increased to 7.7 percent in 1993–94 against a target of 4.7 percent, reflecting revenue shortfalls and expenditure overruns. However, it was reduced again to 6.7 percent in 1994–95.

Indian reforms placed public enterprises in three categories: those with 51 percent public ownership, those with 26 percent public ownership, and those with 0 percent public ownership. But once again, divestiture has been slow despite an awareness that India could retire its public debt through this action. Even where shares have been offered for sale, restrictions have meant weak demand. Moreover, reform has been inhibited by the imperfect labor market plus the problems of closing down inefficient public enterprises. The government, which recognizes that labor turnover is handled more easily in a growing economy where reemployment is possible, is sensitive to the labor issue. Much of the resistance to reform comes from white-collar managers, who do not feel that the rules of the new game have been adequately clarified. Blue-collar workers, on the other hand, seem to understand that they will benefit from the reforms in the long run. In the meantime, the government must move slowly, since each worker employed in the public sector has an average of 19 dependents.[4]

The reforms opened up the manufacturing sector, especially for foreign companies. Despite Indians' complaints about the quantity and pace of investment, foreign domestic investment in India increased tenfold in the early 1990s. That investment could be even greater were India to push more aggressively on the consumer-related deregulation front.

The post-1991 reforms hold out the promise of generating wealth; but can they end the poverty in India that touches 35 percent of a population of almost 1 billion? The very scope of the reforms ensures that they will be criticized, by some for not going far enough and by others for going too far. Those on the left accuse the government of hurting the poor. On the right, nationalists claim that the government merely gave in to the pressure from Western capitalist countries and compromised India's traditional independence. And regardless of reform, the issue of corruption is still pervasive in the Indian political system and affected the outcome of the 1996 election. In the course of the campaign, the Congress Party and former Prime Minister Rao were accused of tolerating corruption by limiting the scope of judicial inquiries. On the other hand, the Rao government was helped by the reputation of its reformist finance minister, Manmohan Singh, for honesty and good sense. By September 1996, Rao was out of Congress and facing a potential trial for corruption and misuse of power.

Despite Rao's fall from grace, the reforms can be given high marks for having stabilized the fiscal imbalances of the central government. They have significantly reduced tariffs, offered full convertibility for current account transactions, and virtually eliminated the import licensing restrictions on intermediate and capital goods. Furthermore, financial markets have been liberalized and banks have more discretion in their lending decisions. India enjoyed a 5.3 percent growth in the GDP in 1994–95—one of the best reform experiences in the world that year and the largest growth since reforms were initiated in 1991.[5]

A word about the comparison between East and South Asia is warranted. Several key differences distinguish the economic paths of countries of East Asia from those of South Asia. First, East Asia's more broadly based income distribution contributed to a lesser gap between the rich and everyone else. Second, savings are crucial to the development of nations, and South Asia has suffered in comparison with East Asia in the percentage of savings relative to the

GDP. "East Asians supported their economic miracle by investing close to two-fifths of their GDP. South Asia, while investing about a fifth of its GDP, financed only two-thirds of it from domestic savings."[6] The difference was made up by foreign assistance and expatriate remittances. Third, the relative frugality of governments in East Asia contrasts with the pattern of overspending in South Asia. For example, large outlays for defense and internal and external debt take up nearly 80 percent of the Pakistani budget, causing large budget deficits. Fourth, exports account for nearly one-tenth of all global exports of low- and middle-income East Asian countries. Thus these countries are better integrated into global trade. They have reserves of near-ly $100 billion, compared with only $15 billion for South Asia. Fifth, human resource development has been dramatically lacking in countries of South Asia, whereas it has surged ahead in East Asia. Programs in education, health, and population control have all declined in South Asia. The case for females is even starker. Successive Pakistani governments have thus far offered only slogans for change; the reality reflects a different picture. Developments in the southern states of Kerala and Karnataka of India, however, have demonstrated the difference that female literacy can make in the overall improvement of social indicators. Sixth, "good governance" contributes significantly to economic development. Good governance includes the capacity to mobilize and to allocate resources efficiently for development and rational decision making with institutional support. Both criteria are essential for attracting foreign investment. Seventh, social harmony reflective of the relative homogeneity of East Asian countries is clearly absent in South Asia with its rich mix of ethnic and culturally pluralistic societies. Current conditions in Karachi, Pakistan, reflect the damage to economic development that comes from long-standing political divisions and arbitrary behavior by political opponents and the government.

THE POLITICAL BASE FOR REFORM

The Rao government stated forcefully that there is no turning back from the reform process. The U.S. government has welcomed that position as an affirmation of the fact that "all major groups, including the opposition," support the shift to a market-based economy.[7] Commerce Department classification of India as one of the top-ten big emerging markets enhances its position as an American trade priority.

Senior U.S. officials continue to press the government of India for American access to the Indian market, in the belief that such access is necessary for India to become an active part of the global market. Many Indians disagree about the extent of access to their market and would prefer to limit foreign investment to much-needed areas such as energy, telecommunications, and infrastructure projects (including ports and roads). Despite the identification of reforms with the Rao government, statements by the Bharatiya Janata Party (BJP) and the United Front governments after the 1996 election promised that reforms will be adhered to. Acknowledging that interest in Indian reforms and their future direction could set the pace for further investment in the country, the short-lived BJP government moved quickly to reassure the world that reforms were irreversible. Leaders of the subsequent United Front government have continued to state the same commitment.

Because Rao and a handful of colleagues set the pace and the quality of the reform process, some worry that it rests on a narrow political base. Others argue that the 1991 reforms are built on consensus as a political necessity, coming as they did when the Congress Party government had only 219 members out of a total of the 544 members in parliament.[8] It took Rao time to build support for reform even within his own party. He moved cautiously because he took office after Rajiv Gandhi's assassination, and he could not afford to be charged with the betrayal of "Nehruvian socialism." Furthermore, Rao could not ignore the fact that the Congress Party would be saddled with the blame for the policies leading to the crises that made reform critical because for much of the time since independence, it had been the party in power.

During the Rajiv Gandhi era, Montek Singh Ahluwalia, the same man who later worked with Finance Minister Manmohan Singh, had foreseen India's economic problems, and he knew that foreign exchange reserves were depleted. However, the minority government of V.P. Singh that took office after the 1989 elections was politically weak. The new prime minister had served as Rajiv Gandhi's minister of finance and was aware of the approaching problems and the need for reform. Ahluwalia continued to work for the prime minister but was hampered by the fact that there was no consensus for reform. Furthermore, the Gulf crisis created great uncertainties; not only were remittances from Indian workers in the Gulf lost, the workers themselves had to be repatriated, and higher fuel prices ensued. Singh's government fell in November 1990. Mr. Chandrashekar headed a weak government while India prepared for elections. Under such conditions, reform was postponed as Rajiv Gandhi, on whom Chandrashekar depended, wanted to wait until after the voting. Gandhi's assassination and the sympathy it engendered brought a stronger Congress Party back to power.

In order to build a base of political support for reform, Rao adopted a gradualist approach to some of the measures demanded by the International Monetary Fund (IMF) and dealt swiftly with others. Measures aimed at the reduction of the fiscal deficit to 5 percent of the GDP were initially enacted over the first two years but stretched to five years. The reduction of tariffs on imported goods has taken over four years, with some work still to be done on duty on consumer goods. The IMF encouraged current account convertibility of the rupee, which was achieved over four years. The reform process proceeded cautiously because of the need to maintain support for it inside India and to limit opposition.

Opposition to the reforms was widespread at first, coming from a sizable sector within industry, organized labor, farmers, and the intelligentsia, groups likely to be hurt to varying degrees by the reforms. The burden on fixed-income groups was disproportionately large and thus the intelligentsia felt aggrieved. Because the free press is a vibrant part of the Indian democracy, there was a good deal of coverage of the reforms and what they would cost those on fixed incomes. Farmers were unhappy at the rising costs of fertilizer, seeds, and the like and the declining chances of continued subsidies that would guarantee reasonable incomes. On fertilizers alone, these subsidies had grown to more than $2 billion annually, an amount that compensated for the fact that their production was only for the domestic market.

India's labor, which had been protected by a strong union movement and a large public sector, was also affected by the reform package. Emphasis on production and profitability meant closing some public industries. The costs of competition from domestic and foreign sources offered challenges for the surviving industries. Conscious of the outcry, the Rao government slowed decisions on the exit policy that set the rules under which labor could be terminated from industries slated to close down. The government understood that the social costs of laying off large numbers were high and moved to strengthen the financial and managerial foundations of state enterprises to give them a chance to compete. Those that were unable to survive could then be closed with less political uproar.

The pace of Indian reforms was, therefore, slower than might have been the case if politics were not "always given priority over economics."[9] The government chose to emphasize transparency and attention getting. Public enthusiasm over reform was kept alive by the workings of the various commissions and committees, the public debate that detailed the advantages and the perils of reforms in the press, and continuous statements from senior officials, including the prime minister.

The gradualist approach also allowed the government time to garner support and to blunt criticism that the reforms violated Indian sovereignty and increased the gap between rich and poor. Rao hoped that the proper sequencing of reforms would allow growth to resume. A slower pace for reforms also helped those adversely affected by them. While keeping international attention focused on the bold steps that he was undertaking, Rao calculated that should he have to move faster, his record would at the very least demonstrate careful calibration and concern for the dislocation caused by the reforms.

All this was not enough. As the Congress Party lost a series of state elections in March 1995, some worried that the election results reflected a lost mandate for change. U.S. companies were concerned about the commitment of the incoming opposition governments to reforms in key states, such as Maharashtra. Private consultations, however, reinforced the message that there would be no turning back on key elements of the reform package.

Consensus favoring reforms emerged early as the chief ministers of Karnataka, Andhra, Maharashtra, Uttar Pradesh, Orissa, and West Bengal (the last has a Marxist government) all endorsed the economic policies of privatization and foreign investment. The majority of these states saw the advantages in reforms after their elections. But in at least two, Uttar Pradesh and West Bengal, local leaders had experienced the benefits of reforms two years earlier.

State government support has been crucial to the overall process. The Rao government pressured the states by insisting that they end their deficits and clear up the arrears owed by state-run service industries for a variety of services. The states' desire to attract foreign investment into their energy and infrastructure projects obliged them to make serious efforts in the direction demanded by the central government. Failing public enterprises were sold when they became economically unattractive. By acting impartially and with single-mindedness, Rao managed to get the process of change through to the states without facing a large revolt.

Reforms at the state level were important because foreign investors had to deal with the union and state governments. State-level issues are noteworthy since financial and institutional weaknesses at that level are holding back further reform and the delivery of infrastructure and social services. States account for nearly 53 percent of the total expenditure of central government and states combined. Indian states receive nearly 60 percent of their total revenue from tax receipts (land revenue and agricultural income tax, state sales tax on trade within states, state excise duty on alcohol, tax on motor vehicles), of which a third is collected on behalf of states by the central government.

States share responsibilities in those areas of the reform process in which they play a key role, such as irrigation and road transport, power, and education. Some states have begun the difficult but important fiscal reform process: strengthening of property taxes in Andhra Pradesh and public enterprise reform in Uttar Pradesh are two such examples. Experts agree that the economic and political balance between the center and the states is shifting toward greater autonomy for the states, which could result in a fragmented approach to national policies where the states are key players. On the other hand, the 1995 agreement on state sales tax harmonization is illustrative of a successful federal/state dialogue.[10]

ACCESS TO U.S. COMPANIES

President Reagan's decision to sign a memorandum of understanding with India on high-technology sales in 1984 opened up economic relations between the countries. Within a decade, economic considerations had become the most dynamic component of the Indo-U.S. relationship.

Yet in the late 1990s, American companies and the U.S. government expect greater access to the Indian consumer goods market than they currently enjoy. Despite the relatively modest size of American investment in India thus far as compared with that elsewhere in Asia, the psychological opening to international investment has been wider because American companies have led the way. Economic relations have energized the Indo-U.S. relationship, and the number of economic exchanges are increasing steadily.

Indian officials point out that there are vast opportunities in the country, where the middle class outnumbers the entire population of the United States. India offers a large consumer market. American companies already interested in India include Coca-Cola, Kellogg, AT&T, Enron, Motorola, McDonald's, KFC, Timex, and Morgan Stanley. Two aspects of the reform package have particular significance for India as an investment market. One is the increased share foreign companies are allowed to hold in joint ventures; this is now set at 51 percent. The second is permission to sell in India under the brand name. Some Indians continue to hope that goods produced in India will be exported to other countries. The joint ventures now being set up will offer India the technology and the capital, along with training of the labor force, that will facilitate Indian access to the international market.

For American investors, India offers an English-speaking, well-educated labor force as well as lower production costs, but opening the country to foreign companies for production there is still a slow process. Decades of protection for domestic producers have made the change even slower. Companies, therefore, still worry about the length of time bureaucrats take even though the government has reduced red tape and the number of approvals traditionally needed under the old system known as "license raj."

Reforms have already made American companies amenable to more risk-taking and have encouraged them toward India. They remain cognizant, however, of political crises and the danger of reversal that the country faces. Accustomed to the American form of government with its four-year presidential term, some American companies have difficulty accepting the fact that the government in Delhi can change overnight through a vote of no confidence. That plus fear of communal riots, unknown in the United States, the rise of Hindu extremism, and financial scandals in the Bombay stock exchange have all served to dampen enthusiasm for deeper U.S. business participation in India.[11]

Some companies, such as General Electric (GE), are investing heavily in India. GE has invested nearly $100 million in areas such as medical equipment, plastics, and appliances. Sales are over $400 million annually and are predicted to double by the year 2000. The GE strategy of focus on India, the Pacific Rim countries, and Mexico is expected to provide 25 percent of its total sales by then. In the field of medical equipment, GE is competing with Siemens and Philips as it seeks a dominant share of a vast market. India's pool of engineers adds to its attractiveness for companies such as GE that want to be able to enlist Indian labor and produce technology for other developing countries.

While Indo-U.S. trade grew to nearly $8 billion in 1996, the high tariffs remaining on imported consumer items have worried American firms that want to do business in India. The government of India points out that since 1991, it has lowered duties sharply on an array of goods and vastly reduced the list of nonimportable items. The maximum 65 percent duty in India is still high when compared with that of other countries but is far lower than its peak rate of 150 percent in 1991–92. Levies on capital goods and equipment range from 25 to 50 percent. Under a phased duty reduction plan, ad valorem import duty rates will be reduced to 0 to 30 percent by the end of 1998.

India also has withdrawn the general condition that dividend repatriation be matched by foreign exchange inflows, except in the case of consumer products. Furthermore, large parts of the restrictive Foreign Exchange Regulation Act have been abandoned.

During his May 1994 visit to the United States, former Prime Minister Rao focused his efforts on publicizing these developments. Beyond the specifics of the reform process and the update provided during the visit, Rao wanted to signal the psychological change that reforms implied—that India would henceforth look for greater investment from American companies and work toward a larger share of their overseas investment. For Rao, changing the investment picture in India was a high-stakes game undertaken in the hope that the resulting economic growth would stabilize support for reform and reduce unemployment. The "human face" of reforms was important to the prime minister, who told economic and political leaders at the World Economic Forum at Davos in 1993 that "governments do not have the right to go overboard and to plunge large numbers of people into mass misery."[12] Thus far, the investment in the capital sector has had little impact on unemployment. With an eye on key state elections, Rao ordered the finance minister to increase subsidies for food and fertilizer, adding to the $18 billion deficit on $49 billion government outlays. Voters were clearly unimpressed because despite the measure, which added "dead weight" on the reforms, the Congress Party suffered heavy losses.[13]

In the past, U.S. concerns with intellectual property rights limited India's access to American technology and created tensions in Indo-U.S. relations. The United States accused India of stealing patents on medicines, food products, and chemicals, and threatened special retaliation under the 301 legislation.[14] Because no laws existed for these areas, Indian companies were able to copy every new product, claiming that the process of manufacture was different and thus outside the purview of patent laws.

India signed on to the 1994 Uruguay Round of General Agreement on Tariffs and Trade (GATT) because it favored a liberalized regime for trade, which is critical for India's exports at a time when a number of its products have become highly competitive in the world market. The devaluation of the rupee made these products cheaper as it made imports more expensive. Farm product exports climbed to their present number-three position, after textiles and gemstones, on the list of top foreign exchange earners. Indian reforms rely on increasing the share of exports in the gross national product. As such, the Reserve Bank of India sold more than 6 billion rupees in 1994 to keep the current rupee-to-dollar ratio.

Since India signed on to GATT, Indian legislation has been modified to match that of the rest of the world. Indian companies, sheltered by past practice, fear that they will be unable to make the switch to a longer patent period of 20 years. They have lobbied hard, claiming that GATT will mean higher costs for medication. They point out that Indian drug prices are low and as a result the Indian pharmaceutical industry does not reap the profits of its counterparts in the developed world. Indeed, profits are less than 2 percent.

American companies interested in India have worked hard to carry the message that, with an untapped market of 890 million people, the country's potential is comparable to that of China. The India Interest Group, an organization of large companies doing business with India formed in 1993, spends its time lobbying administration officials on company projects in India and the general need to help create favorable conditions for U.S. investment and trade. Members point to China, whose human rights policies did not deter the Clinton administration from continuing its most-favored-nation status. They argue that India is important enough to mute criticism regarding child labor laws and crackdowns on unrest in the Punjab and Kashmir. The 1994 Rao visit to the United States was carefully choreographed to emphasize the India Interest Group while he refused to meet with any human rights groups. This visit was a far cry from earlier Indian high-level visits when India was essentially on a blacklist of countries, because of its close ties with the Soviet Union, and was cut off from access to American technology.

Expectations of large-scale American investment initially created a great deal of excitement. Indians later complained that the pace and magnitude did not keep up with U.S. investments elsewhere, especially in China. The death of Commerce Secretary Ron Brown and the preoccupation with reelection by key members of the Clinton administration resulted in a sharp drop in U.S. commercial activity in India. Furthermore, a shortage of domestic capital in India compounded this slowdown and the implementation of previously planned projects.

PAKISTAN'S ECONOMIC PERFORMANCE

If market size is the most important consideration for the United States, then Pakistan will obviously remain a distant second to India in American calculations. The once-intense relationship—which helped end the Soviet occupation of Afghanistan in the 1980s—atrophied badly throughout the early 1990s. The breaking point was Pakistan's nuclear program, which provoked U.S. legislation. Even had there not been a nuclear program, the relationship would have been severely constricted since the end of the Cold War removed the basic rationale that governed 40 years of U.S.-Pakistan relations. Pakistani attempts to project a post–Cold War agenda in which it would serve as a bridge to Central Asia did not convince Washington. Although Pakistan claimed that it could help create new economic possibilities for the United States in Central Asia, continuing conflict in Afghanistan severely limited access through Pakistan and thus its role. Furthermore, while the United States acknowledged that Benazir Bhutto's fears about terrorism and fundamentalism were legitimate, both these issues were drawbacks to American investors. Bhutto lobbied hard for American investment. As we discuss later, her best results came in one of the priority areas, energy.

Pakistani liberalization policies and the search for foreign investment are a legacy of the Nawaz Sharif government. As a businessman, the former prime minister understood that pursuit of international companies was a necessity for Pakistani economic well-being. Although some of his attention-getting schemes—such as the national highway, for which he sought South Korean cooperation, and the privatization of public enterprises—were popular in parts of Pakistan, Benazir Bhutto subsequently reduced their scope. Nawaz Sharif also began to simplify procedures across a broad front, including customs and the free convertibility of the rupee. Generous personal allowances for private individuals to bring back popular consumer items made a dent in the black market and limited customs officials' corruption opportunities. Nawaz Sharif's plan to bring yellow taxis into the country as a means to employ Pakistan's educated youth backfired with charges that over $1 billion had been misspent.

The 1993 elections were less a search for a mandate for change in Pakistan's economic policies than a struggle for political power between adversaries. However, economic issues were important in the elections as both major parties said they favored foreign investment and liberalization of economic policies. The caretaker government of Moeen Qureshi, which followed the Muslim League government of Nawaz Sharif and preceded the PPP win by Benazir Bhutto, undertook measures that led to the IMF relief package for Pakistan. Unencumbered by political and personal considerations, the caretaker government was able to move swiftly in making reforms that it felt were needed immediately, such as increased autonomy for the State Bank of Pakistan and the initiation of taxation on the wealthy, including both the industrial and the agricultural sectors. There was also an attempt to mobilize savings from the more dynamic sectors of the economy, including agriculture. In consultation with the two political parties, the caretaker government expanded reforms to include strong measures in fiscal, monetary, and exchange rate policy. The Bhutto government legislated the continuation of the caretaker government's action regarding the tax on agricultural wealth and the autonomy of the State Bank, albeit in a considerably diluted form. Any future positive response from the IMF required such minimal action, along with trade reform.

Subsequent to the August 1993 reforms, which had been implemented to secure the IMF relief package, the economic picture brightened with the reduction in the overall fiscal deficit and an increase in gross reserves. GDP growth for 1993–94 was 3.8 percent. A devaluation of the rupee by 10 percent along with fiscal and monetary controls helped meet the IMF standby targets. The privatization list of 103 industrial units included two autonomous agencies, the Water and Power Development Authority (WAPDA) and the Pakistan Telecommunication Corporation (PTC). However, though discussed, greater transparency in privatization did not take place.

By 1994, the World Bank acknowledged that there had been "significant progress in the area of structural reform: introduction of measures to liberalize the external trade and payments system; initiation of a wide-scale privatization program; opening up areas previously reserved for the public sector; relaxation of regulations for foreign and domestic investments; adjustment in administered prices; and financial sector reform."[15]

Pakistan's GDP growth was 2.3 percent in 1992–93, 3.8 percent in 1993–94, and 4.7 percent in 1994–95. Manufacturing increases dipped to 4.4 percent in 1994–95, compared with 5.4 percent in 1992–93 and 1993–94. Despite increased foreign portfolio investment, the overall picture did not improve because economic growth did not reach targeted levels in 1994–95. The fiscal deficit and government borrowing exceeded the government's goal, adding to inflation. The inadequacy of the tax base, heavy defense spending, and debt servicing all combined to keep the budget deficits high, above 7 percent of GDP; inflation also remained high, at an annual rate of over 15 percent.

The government proceeded with the reform agenda in the following areas: tax reform, improvements in management of public expenditures, financial sector reform, trade reform, privatization, and further deregulation. Progress in all of the above for 1993–94 was considered impressive by the World Bank, but Pakistan has been judged harshly in the area of governance, where public policy is notoriously uncertain and lacks transparency. With a moribund legislature, there is hardly any accountability in a system that has grown used to the "victor take all" mentality. The country is still overregulated, initiative is shunned, and institutions routinely fail to perform. All of this, added to a sluggish legal system, an outmoded infrastructure, and a growing reputation for corruption, makes Pakistan much less attractive than other markets to foreign investors. If greater transparency, better governance, improved infrastructure, and continued structural reform and macroeconomic stability take place, the pace of foreign direct investment and foreign portfolio investment in Pakistan should speed up.

Bhutto stated during her election campaign that measures to reduce poverty in Pakistan would be a high priority of her government. Toward that end, she undertook to seek improvements in macroeconomic management through a reduction in the fiscal deficit by implementing tax reforms, expenditure programming, and increased domestic resource mobilization. She also accelerated efforts to tackle poverty through sustained economic growth. Her government launched the Social Action Program to improve basic education (particularly for girls), to enhance basic social services and infrastructure with an emphasis on the rural sector, and to reduce population growth. In addition, she sought to promote private-sector activity through privatization, industrial deregulation, and price adjustment and to direct private funds to high-priority areas such as education, environment, and basic infrastructure. The World Bank judged the reform package, as a whole, as improving Pakistan's long-term economic prospects. Poverty reduction appeared possible, provided the government actually implemented its proposals in a timely manner and that the country had access to adequate levels of external financing.[16]

Pakistan's requirement for external financing for 1994–95 and 1995–96 was $4.1 billion a year, of which $3.2 and $2.5 billion a year, respectively, was financed through official aid. Because of the need for aid from external sources, it is important that Pakistan should make known to the world that it has launched a rational economic plan. Setbacks such as those suffered in the 1993 political tussle between the elected prime minister, Nawaz Sharif, and the president hurt that image. The ongoing fighting in Karachi, which has claimed over 2,000 lives, also hurt the Bhutto government's projection of a democratic and modern Pakistan well on the road to economic recovery.

Pakistan's performance in the agricultural sector is always hostage to the weather, as the flooding of 1992 demonstrated. Cotton and wheat production have fallen despite the government's improved procurement and export policies.

The energy sector is of prime importance, and Benazir Bhutto courted American companies to invest in Pakistan's energy projects. She established an energy task force to set the stage for priorities in the energy sector.[17] Private-sector involvement in energy production is expected to relieve the brownouts that hurt Pakistani industrial production and are a normal feature of Pakistani daily life. By 1995, Bhutto's aggressive pursuit of American companies was reaping rewards as several major corporations, including Cogen Technologies, Enron, AT&T, Brown & Root, General Electric Transportation Systems, and Union Texas/Edison, signed up for business in Pakistan.

The petroleum policy of 1994 called for an investment of $20 billion in the next four to five years and outlined financial incentives for investors in both upstream and downstream areas. By simplifying the regulatory framework and offering a monitoring of policy at the highest level, the government hoped to demonstrate its determination to attract private foreign investment in the petroleum sector. Foreign investors have shown their interest in refining facilities and the transportation of petroleum products. In view of Pakistan's need for energy, which is growing at an annual rate of 12 percent, the government's emphasis on this sector appears timely. Most commercial energy in Pakistan is supplied by oil and natural gas. Oil, which meets 40 percent of the energy needs, is mostly imported, with roughly 25 percent produced in the country. Natural gas meets 38 percent of the energy needs and is supplied from domestic gas fields.[18] Because known reserves of natural gas within Pakistan are already nearly fully committed, the country hopes to interest multinationals in pipelines from the neighboring countries of Iran, Qatar, and Turkmenistan.

The visit of Prime Minister Bhutto to the United States in April 1995 focused on the economy. She publicly sought American investment in Pakistan and personally oversaw the signing of several memoranda of understanding and agreements between American companies and her country. She promised the integration of Pakistan into the global economy and special incentives to draw investment there, such as 100 percent ownership, repatriation of capital and profits, and tax exemptions for three to ten years. Her slogan was: "A Pakistan committed to foreign trade, not foreign aid. A Pakistan committed to MOUs [memoranda of understanding] and not IOUs."[19] During her visit, Bhutto made many references to the fact that, increasingly, Pakistan was one of the strongest of Asia's new emerging markets.

Despite the promise of foreign investment, the reality was different. Many of the MOUs signed under Bhutto's supervision in the course of her 1995 visit to the United States did not materialize, and feasibility studies indicated that some of the projects were not even warranted. Other projects were held up because of corruption problems in the Pakistani hierarchy. By 1996, Pakistan's economic picture was bleak. In the second half of 1996, Bhutto turned to the IMF for additional help. The IMF responded by calling for harsh reforms that were bound to be unpopular in a country that was already suffering from a 20 percent inflation rate. Bhutto swallowed the bitter pill and initiated some of the reforms. But by then, the IMF and the World Bank had already found many discrepancies in the figures supplied by the government of Pakistan and insisted on a more intrusive role for the IMF in Pakistani affairs. Future help was contingent on reforms and on performance, both of which were to be closely monitored. Even so, Pakistani officials were sent to Washington to secure loans from the IMF but came back empty-handed. By August 1996, Pakistan was said to possess only "weeks' worth" of foreign exchange. The government had reached an impasse, and rumors of waste and stories of corruption were circulating.

Following the dismissal of the Bhutto government in November 1996 on charges of incompetence and corruption, an interim government was put into place to alleviate the economic and political crises. The appointment of Shahid Javed Burki as economic advisor in the interim government assured that a very competent professional of the highest integrity took charge of a key area. On loan to Pakistan for the three-month stint from the World Bank, Burki was expected to undertake measures of damage control, focus on financial-sector reform, institute some painful cuts, and bring in a cadre of bureaucrats with reputations for serious work. The World Bank came through with a $200 million loan for financial-sector reform. Some of the changes would be implemented as presidential ordinances and thus survive beyond the tenure of the interim government.

The IMF was also asked to increase its standby agreement with Pakistan from $580 to $815 million. The government asked that the agreement, rather than expire at the end of 1996, be extended to September 30, 1997. In this new plan, the full amount would not be offered at the outset. Rather, $160 million would be made available during the tenure of the interim government. The next three tranches would follow in March, June, and September 1997. These would be based on government performance. The IMF included strict regulations in this new agreement, calling for expenditure cuts, a rise in the price of petroleum to 5 percent above the world market price, a rollback on preferential tax on textiles, and the elimination of the 5 percent concessional tax rate to make it a full 10 percent. Pakistan also sought assistance from the United Arab Emirates government for approximately $500 million. Yet with all of these measures in place before the February election, the road ahead is a tough one, requiring any successor government to closely follow the above plan and practice stringent fiscal discipline.

INVESTING IN ENERGY

The energy sector provides a good case to evaluate the performance of the postreform policies of India and Pakistan against their promise. In their effort to speed economic growth and to attract foreign investment, both countries have given priority to the energy sector. The Indian government announced a major change in its power policy because of serious shortages in the domestic capacity and the ever-increasing demand. The Union Power Ministry announced a policy of privatizing the power sector and offered major incentives to foreign investors, including assured terms on equity and waiving of the competitive bidding system on certain phases of energy projects. The government also took the bold step of allowing full ownership of the power plants.

The government of India hopes to achieve a significant increase in the country's electric generation capacity in the next 15 years. It plans to add approximately 60,000 megawatts of electrical power to its current capacity by the year 2000 and over 140,000 megawatts by 2007, a goal that will require nearly $600 billion in investment. In order to reach this goal, the government envisions the building of 67 power plants, for which it is seeking technical expertise and foreign investors.

The energy policy of the Rao government led to the development of private power project proposals worth approximately $25 billion. A dozen American companies are involved in about half of these projects, including the Houston-based Enron Corporation. In 1993, the Indian Federal Investment Promotion Board approved the proposals for seven "fast-track" power projects, all with American investment. U.S. private investment in power generation in India is expected to reach $5 billion to $6 billion by the year 2000.

Recognizing the critical role of energy to foreign investment in India, Secretary of Energy Hazel O'Leary visited Delhi in July 1994; Undersecretary of Commerce Jeffrey Garten visited in November. During her meeting with Rao, O'Leary urged the Indian government to move forward quickly on the seven fast-track projects that were already under way. She emphasized that the projects would serve as models of collaboration for the other 60 power project proposals submitted by U.S. companies. Rao agreed and proposed the establishment of a subcommission to expedite private power projects under the umbrella Indo-U.S. Joint Commission.

During the O'Leary visit, the one-day Indo-U.S. Energy Summit on Cooperation for Sustainable Development allowed the visiting U.S. delegation to unveil a plan of action for cooperation in supplying India with technical expertise and technology. The government of India committed itself to promoting conditions appropriate for smooth economic relations between the two countries. India further pledged that, to satisfy foreign investors, the government would provide counterguarantees for the first several power projects. The five areas of possible cooperation dealt with by the mission were renewable energy, energy efficiency, electrical power production, oil and gas, and nuclear safety.

In the course of the January 1995 visit of Commerce Secretary Ron Brown to India, the U.S.-India Commercial Alliance was established to cover a variety of areas, including energy. Brown was successful in obtaining Indian government counterguarantees for a second fast-track project in Orissa. The Dhabol Power Corporation's (DPC) power station was the first of the fast-track power stations the government approved as part of its new energy policy. Set off the Konkan coast of Maharashtra, the $920 million Enron Dhabol project provides 695 megawatts to the state. It is cited as an example of Indian seriousness in attracting American companies for large projects. DPC is jointly owned by Enron Development Corporation (which has an 80 percent equity stake in the project), General Electric (for turbines, with 10 percent equity), and Bechtel Corporation (with 10 percent equity). DPC won approval from the Indian government in December 1993 and was expected to be a pioneer power project in the country.

The Enron project became mired in controversy soon after the Congress Party's loss of Maharashtra in the March 1995 elections. In August the new state government canceled the $2.9 billion power plant, stating that the contract negotiated by its predecessor was flawed and represented foreign exploitation. Initially ignoring the fact that Enron had spent $300 million by the date of cancellation, the new BJP-Shiv Sena government declared the terms of the agreement to be unduly favorable to the U.S. companies and detrimental to Indian interests. Among the criticisms were the reported lack of transparency in the negotiations, the absence of competitive bidding, and high tariffs. The cancellation occurred after a four-member ministerial committee was appointed by the deputy chief minister of Maharashtra, Gopinath Munde, to review the conditions of the project and issue a verdict that required all contracts to reflect transparency. The U.S. government supported the Enron project and signaled unhappiness with the violation of the sanctity of the negotiated contract. The Energy Department made clear that failure to honor the Enron agreement would damage India's chances of attracting any more U.S. investment in its energy sector.

Enron asked for arbitration and compensation to the tune of $300 million from the government of Maharashtra. Just before the scheduled meeting of the arbitration panel in London in November 1995, Chief Minister Manohar Joshi decided to "revive" the project, appearing willing to review the cancellation after Enron offered on September 19, 1995, to match the lowest electricity tariffs in Maharashtra and to sell 30 percent of its stake in the company to local investors. The Maharashtra government pledged to allow Enron to proceed with the project under the new rates.[20] A change in fuel from distillates to naphtha also helped reduce the costs. Other issues, including the percentage of power produced to be drawn by the state electricity board, which was previously targeted for 90 percent of the power produced, remain unresolved at this time. There was at least a 90-day stoppage in the project, which meant compensation and the resumption of construction and the completion of the project followed only after the consortium leaders approved the new terms under negotiation between the Maharashtra government and the Enron Development Corporation. Additional political repercussions included charges against the state Congress government and the Rao government, which were used by the opposition in the 1996 national election. Renewing the Enron deal with changed terms opened the Congress Party to accusations that it was involved in a poor deal for India. The future of other fast-track projects is clouded even as the Dhabol project finally moves forward after a court settlement in November 1996.

Pakistan too suffers from chronic energy shortages. Electricity consumption is rising 12 percent annually while peak demand for electricity exceeds supply by 21 percent.[21] Pakistan faces a 25 percent shortfall in electricity production and requires an additional 3,000 megawatts (MW) just to deal with present needs. An estimated 14,500 MW will be needed by the year 2000 in order to accommodate industrial growth. Recognizing that power stations cost approximately $1 billion for each 1,000 MW, the Bhutto government sought foreign investment. American companies were encouraged to become involved in a variety of projects, and several MOUs were signed. To make the terms attractive, the government offered a guaranteed bulk tariff of 6.5 cents per kilowatt-hour, which should yield returns of 22 to 25 percent. U.S. investment in the energy sector could become the cornerstone of the burgeoning commercial relationship between the two countries. Pakistan hopes to attract $8 billion from the private sector.

At the invitation of Prime Minister Bhutto, O'Leary visited Pakistan in September 1994 at the head of an official delegation of some 90 U.S. business executives, environmental leaders, and government officials. The mission concluded with the signing of 16 agreements between U.S. companies and Pakistani private and government corporations totaling $4 billion. Three joint statements of intent were also signed, aimed at encouraging bilateral exchange of information and ideas in the fields of energy and environment. The mission focused on six specific areas in Pakistan's energy sector: finance; electricity generation; transmission and distribution; renewable resources; energy efficiency and demand-side management; and oil, gas, and coal.

Among its plans for energy development, Pakistan views the Hub River project as a model for future private power projects. HubCo, a consortium led by the Saudi Arabian company Xenal Industries and Britain's National Power, concluded its $1.6 billion deal with the government of Pakistan in October 1994. HubCo, a 1,292 MW oil-fired plant, is the largest private-sector power project of its kind in Asia and has been under consideration since 1985. To achieve its goal, HubCo negotiated with 11 successive governments.

The project's financing is extremely complicated and relies heavily on the World Bank. Hub's financial arrangements involve 45 banks, international lending agencies, the floating of global depository receipts, and six currencies. Its financiers include National Power, which invested $100 million; international and local equity investors, who contributed $175 million; and international banks, which invested $689 million. Because of Pakistan's overall reliance on the World Bank, that institution's involvement in guaranteeing the loans is meant to assuage the concerns of investors. The Hub project received $589 million from the World Bank and an additional $240 million in guarantees for political risk on the loans taken by foreign banks. The World Bank indicated that its guarantees are not available for future projects and that private banks will have to assume the risk themselves. However, Pakistani government officials remain optimistic that Hub will be the blueprint for future projects because it involved the first successful international equity offer for a power station that had yet to be built, and future projects will be easier to finance.

Few dispute the fact that economic liberalization is here to stay in India and Pakistan, although its pace and scope could be determined by each successive government. Declining popularity of political leaders means turbulent politics. India held its elections in April 1996. Pakistan was not due for one until 1998, but the Bhutto government's dismissal advanced the timetable to February 1997. To enhance prospects for economic well-being, Indian and

Pakistani leaders have reached out toward a less confrontational future. Bhutto felt vulnerable because declining economic assets and sharply reduced performance influenced her ability to govern. Gowda's ability to lead and to deal with the problems in Kashmir could be improved with a nonconfrontational policy with Pakistan. For 50 years the leaders of these two countries said that they were unable to move toward real rapprochement because the people would not allow it. Pakistani elections scheduled for Febuary 1997 are likely to usher in a new era. The new leaders, it is hoped, will thus go down a different path, one that might remove the causes for war and help improve the economic well-being of the people.

5

Policy Choices: A Blueprint for Action

U.S. INTEREST IN AREAS SUCH AS SOUTH ASIA DEMANDS management of regional tensions. That requirement means that relations between India and Pakistan must remain stable. It is also in the American interest that these relations go beyond a state of cold peace to one where collaboration on some fronts changes the dynamic. Despite a record of extensive but sometimes difficult relations with India and Pakistan, future U.S. involvement in these countries is in the American interest for a number of reasons.

1. Both states are nuclear weapons–capable, and American nonproliferation interests are directly involved.

2. China's long history of relations with India and Pakistan, its importance to the region as a whole, and America's concern about China's foreign interests necessitates continued American involvement in the region.

3. As the region is a close geographic neighbor of the Persian Gulf, the United States must keep abreast of events there and their direct implications for the Gulf.

4. The United States can only be helped by peace and security in the region and hindered by any chaos that might ensue as a result of another war between India and Pakistan, with their combined population of more than 1 billion people and two of the largest and best-trained armies in the region.

5. The American commitment to democracy and human rights mandates that it work to promote this ideal in the region.

6. America's economic relations with India and Pakistan also warrant government involvement. American companies have pledged $7 billion in future investment in India and over $2 billion in Pakistan.

7. In the absence of superpower competition, U.S. interests can be advanced at a lower cost.

Peace between India and Pakistan is of overarching importance for all these reasons, which is why U.S. assistance in Indo-Pak normalization is important.

THE UNITED STATES AND DOMESTIC DEVELOPMENTS: PERCEPTIONS AND EXPECTATIONS

In some ways, it is relatively easy for the United States to engage the leaders of India and Pakistan on most issues because of their belief that the United States has strong views on subcontinental matters and thus is an interested party. U.S. interest in democracy is assumed. Indians view their own commitment to democracy as a natural point of convergence and are puzzled at what they perceive as the slow momentum in their relations with the United States. Related to the question of democracy is the question of political stability. The political, ethnic, and social diversity of both India and Pakistan requires a democratic model if stability is to be achieved. In India, democracy is an established fact, notwithstanding challenges that periodically arise in various parts of the country. Pakistan is different. Despite statements that the army is no longer interested in a power takeover and that the existing division of power suits the military, there are lingering Pakistani suspicions that martial law may be just around the corner. A democratic Pakistan requires a responsible party in power and a viable opposition that plays within the rules of the political game. However, the absence of rules and the personalization of politics in the country militate against this scenario.

Despite an ambivalence regarding the United States, most Pakistanis believe that any government that comes to power must have America's blessing. Similarly, Pakistanis assume that the United States can make and unmake governments at will and often does so. They dismiss without debate the observation that such expectations exaggerate the role that South Asia plays in American policy. At the same time, they credit U.S. support for democracy with having prevented further encroachment by the military against the political system.

From the perspective of the United States, the march of religious fundamentalism threatens regional stability. The rise of religious fervor in India and Pakistan will affect their future as both countries try to harness the energies of their people and propel them into the next century. The advent of a more Islamic state in Pakistan and the functional blurring of the line between state and religion is a legacy of the Zia era. Pakistan has become a more conservative nation, where the decline in the performance of political institutions has facilitated a larger role for the religious elements. Despite its inability to win elections, the religious right remains a potentially important force because of the simplicity of its message, its superior organization, and popular resentment of the poor performance of most Pakistani politicians, both in and out of power.

Right-wing Hindu fundamentalist political parties in India also threaten difficulties for the future as they remain bent on politics of confrontation with the large Muslim population. Such parties suspect Muslims of being nothing more than a front for Pakistan, despite the fact that they are distinctly Indian.

Closely related to the goal of stability is the ability of the political system to manage change. Elections reflect an expression of the will of the people, and the United States is perceived as having become less tolerant of authoritarian regimes in general and more consistent in supporting democracy. South Asians have come to accept problems in the course of implementing political change, whether it is through the electoral process or as a consequence of ethnic complexity that creates tensions in the relationship between the central governments and constituent states.

South Asians routinely assign a greater role for the United States in regional affairs than is warranted, which surfaces as charges of interference in internal affairs. For example, in the course of the Gates mission to India and Pakistan in May 1990, the deputy national security advisor did not meet with Prime Minister Benazir Bhutto, who was away on a previously scheduled trip abroad. Critics charged that by coming to Pakistan at such a time and meeting only with nonelected leaders—the president (who is elected indirectly) and the chief of army staff—the United States actively undercut democracy in Pakistan. Although Gates felt that Bhutto made herself unavailable and the crisis required urgent talks with available officials,[1] some in Pakistan felt that the United States did not consider it necessary to engage the elected prime minister on nonproliferation and thus signaled that the real arbiters of power in Pakistan were the president and the military. Some believe this contributed directly to the dismissal of the first Benazir Bhutto government (by ending the myth that she was the chosen interlocutor for the United States) and the subsequent disbanding of the National Assembly.

While U.S. interest in the region continues, American political involvement in the domestic affairs of the subcontinent via pressure from Washington on a range of domestic issues is limited. However, the presence of a growing and active South Asian community in the United States, now numbering nearly 1 million, compels some attention within the U.S. policy community and in Congress. An active and largely professional group, these new U.S. citizens stay in touch with their representatives in Congress and ask for greater scrutiny on matters of choice. The community functions as a political action committee, supporting issues of concern to the group and raising funds for the campaigns of favored senators or congressmen. However, the overall effectiveness of this group in influencing American policy is greatly reduced because of its tendency to replay the tensions of South Asia in the United States.

U.S. support for democracy is more sustainable in today's South Asia, where there is strong support for democracy. While democracy is indeed welcome, the involvement of the region's intelligence agencies in domestic and foreign affairs challenges it. Often at variance with the political leadership, these institutions are in a position to distort reality and to play the role of kingmaker as their leaders push their own agendas. The intelligence agencies respond to a different set of issues in the making of foreign policy than does the elected leadership. The intelligence agencies of India and Pakistan have fed paranoia about each other and have engaged in cross-border interference with potentially serious consequences for the overall bilateral relationship. Theirs is a dangerous game. They do not have a stake in the maintenance of reasonable relations between their respective countries and, at best, prefer the state of cold peace. They have reinforced the tendencies of the foreign offices in Delhi, and particularly in Islamabad, to be strongly and actively against Indo-Pak normalization. Even when the political leadership is forward-leaning, the bureaucrats in the respective foreign services are unwilling to bend from their hard-line positions.

SUMMARY FINDINGS

First, American interest in South Asia tends to drop dramatically between periods of crisis. The U.S. attention span has been notably short-lived, triggered by crisis conditions and lasting mostly for the duration of a crisis. The 1962 Sino-Indian war, the 1965 Indo-Pakistan war, the 1971 Indo-Pakistan war over Bangladesh, the 1979 Soviet invasion of Afghanistan (U.S. paid attention only long enough to expel the Soviets, which took ten years), and the Gates mission to avert another war over Kashmir all illustrate this point. Considered and constructive engagement by the United States between crises might have better guaranteed peaceful and productive relationships in the subcontinent.

Second, the Cold War provided the lens through which the United States viewed India and Pakistan. The primary reason for that was the proximity of the subcontinent to the former Soviet Union and China, both of which sought close ties and offered assistance. Even as it competed for South Asia with the Communist countries, the United States knowingly allowed a larger role for China and the Soviet Union in South Asia than it was ready to play itself. Soviet mediation at Tashkent in ending the 1965 Indo-Pakistan war is a case in point. At other times, Washington used special relationships for its own purpose—such as the role of Pakistan as a conduit to China in the secret Kissinger mission and the subsequent normalization of Sino-American relations.

Third, the U.S. relationship with the subcontinent is complicated by an asymmetry in perceptions. While the United States looms large in terms of its importance in the minds of the region's leaders and populace, South Asia, in contrast, has not normally been a significant concern for American policy makers. One consequence has been that each stated U.S. interest and policy goal in South Asia gets magnified in regional minds. For example, an interest in access to the oil resources of the Persian Gulf is taken in Pakistan as indicative of the American desire to control the area via Pakistan with a naval base along the Baluchistan coastline. In India, many domestic developments are seen to reflect American preferences and policies. The end of the Cold War and the fact that the United States is the only remaining superpower has further exaggerated the tendency to give each official American statement great weight. Reactions to the various Clinton administration statements on Kashmir are a case in point.

Fourth, it remains unwise for the United States to ignore developments in India and Pakistan, an area with a population of over 1 billion, adjacent to a region considered "vital" to American interests. The Gulf War demonstrated ways in which the area comprising the Persian Gulf and South Asia can influence American policy. India and Pakistan each have large standing armies, sophisticated air forces, and naval capabilities. While India has a vast numerical and technical advantage, Pakistan is also well armed. In addition, each is thought to be nuclear weapons–capable.

Fifth, both India and Pakistan provide access for American goods and technology. Economic relations are based on a mutuality of interest and can be expected to flourish. Both countries have eagerly turned to the United States for trade and investment and have made policy changes to try to ensure a brighter future. Their economic liberalization policies are a result of considered judgment in favor of entering the global market. While India and Pakistan are less significant to overall U.S. trade, the United States looms large in their scopes.

CLOSING OUT THE DECADE

We end with a look at U.S. policy options at the end of the decade. What policies are likely to propel American relations with India and Pakistan into the next millennium?

From the American perspective, it is difficult to totally isolate relations with India from attendant issues in Indo-Pakistan bilateral relations. For example, another Indo-Pak war could wipe out foreign investors' interest in India. Hence, Pakistan will continue to figure in U.S. consideration of the region, a fact that may not please India. American interests in India are not identical to those in Pakistan. Thus, U.S. South Asian policy cannot and must not be made from the two South Asian capitals.

Economic relations provide the glue that binds the U.S. relationship in the subcontinent, particularly with India. The Commerce Department has recognized India as one of a special group of nations. American companies are interested in the subcontinent on the assumption that economic liberalization is here to stay.

U.S. support for economic collaboration between India and Pakistan is important for its success. Traditional wariness, particularly on the part of Pakistan (President Zia once said to the author: "Pakistan's fascination with all things Indian would lead to it getting swamped if controls are lifted!") makes economic openings difficult without U.S. encouragement. Since 1994, economic arguments have won out over political differences a number of times, as India and Pakistan entered into a number of agreements for short-term cooperation and trade. Such examples of collaboration are expanding as the informal trade between the two has reached over $2 billion dollars, although much of that is via third countries. Under GATT, India and Pakistan must exchange most-favored-nation trade status, which will eventually force an end to the barriers for direct trade that have been in place for decades. India supports open trade and most-favored-nation status for Pakistan. A number of lobbies for such trade are growing in Pakistan, while those who oppose it increase pressure on the government to continue protection of industries by withholding most-favored-nation status from India.

U.S. support could further economic confidence-building measures between India and Pakistan. Such support would make it easier for the two countries to reach out toward an economic future where collaboration is more of a pattern. The United States can make cooperation easier in a variety of ways. For example, increased incentives for cooperation can be offered for joint Indo-Pakistan projects through the U.S. Overseas Private Investment Cooperation or through the Export-Import Bank. Collaborative projects should receive priority. In other words, the United States should put a premium on cooperation as an active component of its South Asian policy. The involvement of American companies in joint projects offers the companies a larger market, gives India and Pakistan greater confidence in joint ventures, and creates a peace dividend. The United States should encourage other countries that are economically important to India and Pakistan, such as Japan, to stress economic collaboration and support three-way investment projects.

Support from multilateral institutions for joint economic projects offers a powerful symbol of changed policies. Multilateral institutions should be at the forefront encouraging collaboration, and the United States should take the lead in the governing councils of the World Bank in pushing for a change. The Bank can underwrite some of the initial projects where investor confidence in joint projects is shaky, as it has already done in the Hub River project in Pakistan. A small percentage of the funds allocated for India and Pakistan ought to be specifically marked for joint projects. Progress on implementing joint projects should be the benchmark for bilateral loans from the World Bank to India or Pakistan. The bank tends to be resistant to bold thinking on Indo-Pakistan issues, and American leadership will be critical to new ideas on the subject.

Several regional states have adopted free trade zones. It makes sense that India and Pakistan also try to form one where they could demonstrate cooperative efforts through joint manufacturing and export. Such goods could be imported into the two countries without tariffs. Pakistani manufacturers who fear competition from Indian goods would be better able to deal with these sorts of joint ventures. A joint board of oversight would create institutional links between the two countries.

The subcontinent is already beginning to break out of its isolation in terms of closer ventures with its neighboring regions. For example, India is beginning a dialogue with members of the Association of Southeast Asian Nations (ASEAN) to find ways of enhancing economic ties. In the west, a number of joint projects are under active consideration; some of the most ambitious involve the building of a series of gas pipelines bringing Central Asian and Persian Gulf gas through Pakistan to India. Other areas, such as railroads, offer avenues for cooperation for rebuilding the infrastructure that is in desperate shape on both sides of the Indo-Pakistan border. These types of projects will require external financing, and the U.S. attitude will be an important consideration to potential investors.

Other areas may exist where cooperation is possible and other players can assist in putting the agenda forward.[2]

Nuclear policies of India and Pakistan impinge on U.S. efforts to curb further development of the nuclear weapons option by either state. As such, a discussion of these efforts for the rest of the decade and beyond is important. The United States has helped keep down the level of the Indian and Pakistani nuclear weapons programs, but it has failed to eliminate them. Threats and cutoff of assistance have not led to a rollback of the Pakistani program. Neither have the incentives, such as a large program of security and economic assistance.

The underlying sense of insecurity that forces the maintenance of a nuclear weapons option, no matter how ambiguous, is likely to continue. India will continue to believe that prudent action dictates that it maintain its own limited nuclear capability to defend itself against China, with its large nuclear arsenal. In a wider context, Delhi will push for some indications of nondiscriminatory global disarmament beyond current U.S. treaties with Russia because of the implications of global measures for the Chinese nuclear capability. Pakistan's focus on the Indian program and India's conventional arms superiority will continue to build support for its nuclear weapons program. In other words, the nuclear option, even if it is "nonweaponized," will be seen as comforting and at the current level even affordable. Additionally, to a certain extent, the prestige factor will lead nuclear hawks in India and Pakistan to continue to push such a policy.

India believes arrangements such as the NPT or the Comprehensive Test Ban Treaty (CTBT), under discussion, are discriminatory as they perpetuate the unequal status between the nuclear haves and have-nots. That view is not going to change. According to this view, there must be global disarmament, which would eliminate the threat and thus the need for nuclear weapons. In their discussions with senior U.S. officials, Indian leaders have pointed to Article VI of the NPT, which calls upon the parties to engage in good-faith negotiations for the cessation of the nuclear race and for a treaty on general and complete disarmament.[3] Similar arguments for global disarmament accompany India's unwillingness to become a party to the CTBT. Pakistan's position that it will agree to anything that India does regarding the CTBT sidelines for the present the difficulties inherent in dealing with the domestic support for the nuclear option to provide continued protection against a superior threat from India.

India continues its argument for a global nondiscriminatory regime for disarmament in its discussions for arms control measures, such as the CTBT. Pointing to the restraint in Indian development, New Delhi has insisted that the nuclear weapons states move forward with a time-bound program for eliminating their arsenals. Anything less is considered partial, and India is said to be under no obligation to give up its limited nuclear option. The attempt to engage India and Pakistan in future dialogue must involve a full range of options, starting with the assumption that, like other states, India and Pakistan believe that their nonweaponized deterrent buys them insurance against a more powerful potential enemy. Thus, a focus on the larger security picture in the subcontinent is important to the overall effort. Such an effort can begin with the regional talks that were proposed by the United States in 1991. If India needs greater attendance at the talks than the United States finds comfortable (since the Indians want to include Iran, Iraq, and Saudi Arabia), a compromise could be found in creating two simultaneous sets of talks each with a subset of regional actors. While such a grouping may not lead to speedy action, it will bring up some serious issues of concern such as: under what conditions will India and Pakistan feel more secure; how far are they willing to go beyond mere rhetoric—are they willing to consider a no-first-use pledge in a regional context with external positive security assurances built in; how important is domestic concern for continuation of the present policy; what is their sense of timing for a changed set of priorities in their relations with each other; how far are they prepared to move toward increasing transparency of existing arsenals that retains their current posture but limits their expansion; what verification measures, if any, are obtainable; can a phased approach be fashioned that incorporates these concerns? American agreement to the expanded list of participants will help deflect the criticism that the United States pushes nonproliferation only if it can always have its own way.

It is time to reengage India and Pakistan on the U.S. proposal for broader talks on South Asia and nuclear issues pertaining to the region. Such a discussion is important for freezing the current status of the nuclear capability of both countries. Several difficulties exist in furthering such a dialogue, but they may be overcome through sustained effort. First, after the end of the Cold War and in the early phase of the Russian need for the United States (which India saw firsthand as a member of the Security Council), India is not at all certain of the pressures it might face in a regional forum. On the other hand, China is expected to remain a supporter of Pakistan. Second, there are many versions of the list of potential members of such a forum. Having started with only five (India, Pakistan, China, Russia, and the United States), the group kept expanding to include major European powers, Japan, and even some of the former Soviet republics, such as Kazakhstan, which makes the body too large to focus effectively on the subcontinent. Third, there is a sense of unhappiness in India over its perceptions of a lack of American "evenhandedness" on nuclear issues between India and Pakistan; many consider this attitude insulting because they see India's deliberate policy to limit its nuclear weapons program after 1974 as being patently different from the Pakistani position. Pakistan reacts to the same U.S. policy as a serious letdown, charging that years of friendship did not earn it a special place in the U.S. scheme of things. American interest in finding some way beyond the current impasse has led to several ideas on how the dialogue can move forward.[4]

U.S. policy has shifted its focus from its earlier emphasis on working to limit Pakistani nuclear gains in the bilateral and in the regional contexts to one where there is an acceptance of the reality that Pakistan has limited nuclear capability. In this context, Washington works to ensure that Pakistan's program does not proceed further and does not receive any technology or other form of assistance from any other state. At the same time, Pakistan is offered some incentives for following a policy that limits confrontation with the United States over the nuclear weapons program, such as the Brown amendment, signed into law in 1996, which allows the renewal of some forms of economic assistance to the country. Along these lines, the United States must try to keep Pakistani policy friendly toward the United States and increase marginally its rewards for subscribing to some of the important remaining goals of the U.S. nonproliferation effort in the subcontinent, namely, nontesting, nondeployment, and nontransfer of nuclear weapons.

For the future, U.S. policy at a minimum will continue to call for a freeze of the nuclear programs of India and Pakistan at the lowest level of strategic credibility. Even with a freeze, current American legislation precludes cooperating with these states on all nuclear-related matters. The Brown amendment to the Pressler legislation is a limited attempt to free up certain payments and to return equipment sent for repairs to the United States and already paid for by Pakistan. Limited economic help, particularly in the social sector, also can flow. Military and nuclear-related assistance remains prohibited. Such a policy makes sense in order to protect U.S. interest in limiting the development of a full-fledged Indo-Pak nuclear weapons capability. Thus far, restraint is not simply a question of enlightened self-interest but results also from an awareness in both India and Pakistan that severe penalties could result should they fully develop their nuclear programs. These penalties would go beyond the impact on bilateral relations with the United States and begin to influence the actions of multilateral agencies from which both nations borrow heavily. U.S.

legislation under Section 102(b)(2) of the Nuclear Proliferation Prevention Act of April 30, 1994, expressly applies sanctions if India and Pakistan were to detonate, transfer, or receive design components or information intended for the development or manufacture of a nuclear explosive device. These sanctions include the extension of any loan or financial or technical assistance to that country by any international financial institution. The law also prohibits any U.S. bank from making any loan or providing any credit, except for food purchases or agricultural commodities. There is a cumbersome waiver that the president may exercise, but no state can presume that such a waiver will be forthcoming.

While arms control specialists push for a three-tiered process to cap, roll back, and eliminate the nuclear weapons programs in India and Pakistan, regional experts believe that proliferation is a fact of life that has to be accepted until both states achieve normalization. The "nonweaponized" deterrence status of India and Pakistan is assumed to be a lasting one, given the disincentives against exercising an open nuclear weapons option. Such a "cover" enables Indian political leaders to deal with pressures to move its nuclear programs forward as a symbol of scientific and military parity with China. Nuclear hawks will ask why the government is not meeting the Chinese threat. (India does not really need much beyond its current program to deal with Pakistan.) Rajiv Gandhi acknowledged that the Pressler certification helped keep nuclear hawks at bay even in India, and the former prime minister is said to have stated that otherwise they "would bankrupt us."[5] Similarly, American legislation that precludes a full-fledged nuclear option reduces pressure on Pakistani political leaders to put out large sums from an already strained budget for the nuclear weapons program. Both countries have the technical capability to continue their programs. However, political leaders recognize the larger need for good relations with the United States and use American legislation as a necessary "fig leaf" to rein in the hawks in their respective states. These nuclear hawks believe that only a full-fledged nuclear weapons option can provide a guarantee of national independence and territorial integrity. The task of the political leaders will be made much harder if the

United States takes away the cover they need in order not to be accused of selling out the national interest.

In hindsight, it might have been better to go for some form of international guarantees or "positive security assurances" right after China's testing of its first nuclear weapon. By then a certain amount of symmetry had been achieved; all major post–World War II powers had the bomb, the talisman of the modern era. Even after the Indians set off their "peaceful nuclear explosion" in 1974, guarantees against nuclear blackmail could still have been instituted that may have precluded the Pakistani program, particularly as that country's foreign minister went to Washington in that year unsuccessfully looking for just such a promise.

Despite the decline in the fortunes of the United Nations, guarantees could still be fashioned through it. Among other things, Security Council resolution 255, passed on June 19, 1968, asks parties to the Nonproliferation Treaty to "provide or support immediate assistance to any non-nuclear weapon state party to the NPT that is a victim of an act or an object of a threat of aggression in which nuclear weapons are used." The key here is the timeliness of the international response so that states that do not develop a nuclear capability can deter attack by a nuclear state. Furthermore, the United Nations could be involved in verification procedures in future nonproliferation agreements.[6]

Any future attempts to manage nuclear proliferation in the subcontinent will require involving other relevant states, such as Germany and Japan. Both are in a position to demonstrate the advantages of nonnuclear status and the prestige that accrues from economic performance. While their cases are not parallel with those of India and Pakistan, given the U.S. nuclear umbrella, they represent a postwar policy that focused on economic factors. Representative packages of economic incentives may show India and Pakistan the benefits of political rapprochement. ASEAN members offer another set of states where economic prowess has led to major advancement and where the push for a nonnuclear weapons zone has become a reality.

In the case of India and Pakistan, institution-building through confidence-building measures is urgently needed. The situation in early 1990 demonstrated the ever-present danger of accidental war. While a hot line exists for use in emergencies, it is subject to delays or to nonuse in exactly those situations where it could do some good. Another confidence-building measure could be the setting up of a joint risk reduction center that could start by dealing with conventional threats—since presumably neither country would launch a nuclear attack without some major justification. The United States developed a great deal of expertise in the East-West context, and many arms control experts could help in the areas of monitoring, verification, information sharing and transparency. The United States can play an important role in deterrence through correction of misperceptions based on faulty intelligence.

It is important that India and Pakistan demonstrate to the international community that they do not remain mired in animosities of the past and can take some lead in matters critical to their future. Chemical weapons are outside the purview of development, since both states are signatories to the Chemical Weapons Convention, which has already been ratified by India. This may be a good area for the development of regional verification centers, perhaps under SAARC.

Despite frequent downturns in relations between India and Pakistan, both have honored past agreements. Two examples are the Indus River water-sharing agreement and the agreement not to attack each other's nuclear facilities. Additional areas for future cooperation include implementation of already agreed items, such as provisions of the Chemical Weapons Convention and nonattack on nuclear facilities; expansion of agreed areas, such as joint attendance at IAEA seminars on nuclear safety, compliance, and verification of agreements; and adoption of additional agreements that build institutional links, such as joint monitoring of airspace in some critical areas for border violations, invitation to each other's military exercises, and military exchanges to staff colleges.

A succession of U.S. administrations have dealt with the penalties of proliferation. More focus is needed in providing incentives for India and Pakistan to engage with each other and with the United States in beginning a serious dialogue that can meet the goal of a secure South Asia. Sustained American interest is critical to the involvement of China and Russia, both of which are part of the proliferation equation in the subcontinent.

KASHMIR

The Clinton administration is quietly putting out the word that it would like to do something on Kashmir in its second administration. Such sentiments reflect the belief that there cannot be real peace and stability in the subcontinent until this core issue is resolved. Pakistan has said that the most immediate threat to such a relationship comes from the Kashmir dispute and has pressed for action on the basis of what it believes are India's human rights violations in Kashmir. Islamabad views any U.S. refusal to get closely involved in Kashmir as a lapse of responsibility. The new government of Deve Gowda in New Delhi says that Kashmir will be allowed the maximum level of autonomy within the Indian constitution. It is far from clear whether his government has sufficient votes in Parliament to translate the pronouncements into policy. Given his reliance on the Congress Party for support, any major deviation from the Rao approach may be difficult to sustain. In any case, autonomy may have been sufficient before 1989 but may not now be an adequate guarantee of calm in Kashmir.

The future of the Kashmir issue remains clouded by the fact that all sides are dug in to their respective positions. India is adamant that there can be no shift from the fundamental position that Kashmir will remain an integral part of that country. A change in that status is said to strike at the very nature of the Indian system with implications for the secular state. For India, the problems inside Kashmir are a direct consequence of the assistance Pakistan provided to the militants. Deprived of such help, Indians feel that the problem could be resolved after new elections. Pakistan has argued that since 1989 there has been a new reality inside Kashmir and that India has to accept the desire of the Kashmiris for change. Yet Pakistan itself has not faced up to the new reality that Kashmiris on both sides of the line of control may opt for independence; the self-determination offered by the United Nations no longer adequately measures the true will of the Kashmiris.

So long as the United States supports human rights as one of the priority issues in its foreign policy and problems continue in Kashmir, some attention to the situation in that state will be warranted. In the future, it will be difficult to discuss U.S. human rights policy in the subcontinent without some discussion of Kashmir. These discussions will be complicated by the Indian belief that U.S. and Indian approaches to human rights may be different. India believes that after the United States was willing to bypass human rights issues in China in order for trade and investments to continue, it cannot pressure India regarding Kashmir. The record of violations of human rights in Kashmir has been documented. According to one analysis, in the five and a half years since the Kashmiri insurgents have waged war against the Indian state, the Indian government has deployed "hundreds of thousands of security forces across Kashmir in a brutal counterinsurgency that has left tens of thousands dead."[7] Lack of access to Kashmir by human rights agencies makes Indian claims impossible to monitor. In the meantime, U.S. policy alternates between congressional threats of hearings and executive branch emphasis on "quiet" (and sporadic) diplomacy.[8] The United States has to put human rights violations in Kashmir on its bilateral agenda and press India to open the state to the monitoring agencies. With Pakistan, the United States must continue to insist that terrorism from any source will not be tolerated.

Under present conditions, goodwill notwithstanding, the United States can play only a limited role in resolving the dispute in Kashmir. To win greater U.S. involvement, Pakistan will have to make a better case on the international scene. India will have to pay higher costs for its present policy—a possibly successful Kashmiri case at the Human Rights Commission—and the Kashmiris will need to have a more unified vision of their future. Until some of these events take place, U.S. involvement can be only marginally useful. Furthermore Washington's effort to settle the differences must be part of an overall package of policy options toward India and Pakistan taking U.S. involvement into the next century. The basic premise for U.S. engagement must be the desire to help solve the crises that stand in the way of a permanent and productive peace between India and Pakistan.

Notes

INTRODUCTION

1. For a discussion of the complicated relationship between Jawaharlal Nehru and American officials, see Dennis Kux, *India and the United States: Estranged Democracies, 1941–1991* (Thousand Oaks, CA: Sage Publications, 1994).
2. Cited in the Asia Society Report by Devin T. Hagarty, *Preventing Nuclear Proliferation in South Asia* (New York, NY: The Asia Society, 1995), p. 4.
3. So named because there was no direct contact between the communist government in Kabul and the government of Pakistan. Instead, the special representative of the secretary-general shuttled between the various parties—the United States, the Soviet Union, the Kabul regime, and Pakistan.

CHAPTER 1

1. The Indian constitution stipulates that the central government has the supreme authority on matters of national importance such as defense, foreign affairs, banking duties, and taxation. For a detailed discussion of union/state relations, see Robert Hardgrave, Jr., and Stanley Kochanek, *India: Government and Politics in a Developing Nation*, 4th ed. (New York, NY: Harcourt Brace Jovanovich, 1986). For a history of early Indian politics, see Judith Brown, *Modern India: The Origins of an Asian Democracy* (New York, NY: Oxford

University Press, 1990); and Paul Brass, *The Politics of India since Independence*, 2nd ed. (New York, NY: Cambridge University Press, 1995).

2. For insights regarding the development of the Indian military, see Stephen Rosen, "Military Effectiveness: Why Society Matters," *International Security* 19, no. 4 (Spring 1995), pp. 5–31, and its parent study, *Social Structures and Strategies: India and Its Armies* (Ithaca, NY: Cornell University Press, forthcoming).
3. Proclamation of emergency under article 352 of the constitution was issued on June 25, 1975. Opposition politicians were arrested, civil rights were suspended, and the press was censored. Additional measures were enacted later that year, including the imprisonment of individuals without reason and forced sterilization. The emergency was lifted in January 1977.
4. The 1970 election resulted in a sweep of all electoral votes in East Pakistan by the Awami League under Mujibur Rahman. Zulfikar Ali Bhutto's Pakistan People's Party received the bulk of the votes in West Pakistan. Mujibur Rahman and his Awami League, who won the larger number of votes, ought to have formed a government; however, Bhutto and the Pakistan army were not willing to relinquish power to him. The result was a total deadlock between the two wings of the country and the two populist leaders.
5. For the best analysis of the Bhutto years, see Shahid Javed Burki, *Pakistan under Bhutto, 1971–1977* (New York, NY: St. Martin's Press, 1980).
6. Bhutto subsequently was charged with ordering the murder of a political opponent. He was tried and hanged on April 4, 1979.
7. *Introduction of Islamic Law: Address to the Nation* (Islamabad: Government of Pakistan Press, 1979), p. 12.
8. For a detailed account of domestic politics in the Zia years, see General A. K. Arif, *Working with Zia: Pakistan's Power Politics, 1977–1988* (Karachi: Oxford University Press, 1995).

CHAPTER 2

1. The process of partition of India was to be decided by a referendum in the Muslim areas on whether the populace wished to remain in India or become a part of Pakistan; the result was the formation of Pakistan in two wings separated by a thousand miles of Indian territory. Kashmir, with a Muslim majority, was ruled by a Hindu maharaja and was due for a referendum. After a government-inspired attack by Pathan tribesmen from Pakistan, the maharaja opted for India. In 1948 India took the case to the United Nations, where the Security Council voted to ascertain the wishes of the Kashmiris regarding which country they desired to be part of. That resolution remains on the books but the issue is inactive.
2. See Dennis Kux, *India and the United States: Estranged Democracies, 1941–1991* (Thousand Oaks, CA: Sage Publications, 1994).
3. Herbert G. Hagerty, "United States Assistance to Pakistan," in Leo Rose, ed., *United States–Pakistan Relations* (Berkeley, CA: University of California Press, 1987).
4. In 1962, Sino-Soviet tensions had yet to surface in their full ferocity. Therefore, India worried that help from Moscow might be problematic. However, the Soviets came through with some military supplies, much to the dismay of China.

5. The United States provided $80 million in assistance in the form of radars and equipment designed for high-altitude warfare. For Pakistan, the psychological impact of the aid was greater than its material value.
6. Lawrence Ziring, *The Ayub Khan Era: Politics in Pakistan, 1958–1969* (Syracuse, NY: Syracuse University Press, 1971) p. 52.
7. G. W. Chaudhury, *India, Pakistan, Bangladesh and the Major Powers* (New York, NY: The Free Press, 1975), p. 121.
8. Henry Kissinger, *White House Years* (Boston, MA: Little, Brown, 1979), p. 856.
9. "The Friendship Treaty with India," *Pravda*, Aug. 12, 1971, in *Current Digest of the Soviet Press* 23, no. 32, pp. 5–6.
10. For the best American account of the 1971 war, see Leo Rose and Richard Sisson, *War and Secession: Pakistan, India, and the Creation of Bangladesh* (Berkeley, CA: University of California Press, 1990).
11. The Soviet invasion helped consolidate the U.S. relationship with China, a worry in Moscow and an "obsession" with Mrs. Gandhi, according to some. See Ajoy Sinha, *Indo-U.S. Relations* (New Delhi: Janakai Prakashan Publishers, 1994), p. 267.
12. The Food for Peace program, under the 1954 Agricultural and Trade Development Assistance Act, is better known as Public Law 480 (PL-480). Amended in 1966, it is aimed at combating hunger. The United States lends money at below-market terms to foreign nations to purchase American farm products. Under Title II, farm commodities are also donated to governments friendly to the United States. A portion of the funds raised through food sales is applied toward agricultural development initiatives to improve indigenous food production.
13. Speaking to the Foreign Correspondents' Association of South Asia, New Delhi, Dec. 10, 1985.
14. Speech by Donald Fortier, deputy national security advisor, at Dean Witter, New York, Feb. 25, 1985.
15. Richard P. Cronin, "Congress and Arms Sales and Security Assistance to Pakistan," U.S. House of Representatives, Committee on Foreign Affairs, *Congress and Foreign Policy—1981* (Washington, DC: U.S. Government Printing Office, 1982), pp. 103–114.
16. Hedrick Smith, "Analysis of Carter's State of the Union Address," *The New York Times*, Jan. 24, 1980, p. 1.
17. For an excellent account of the details of the Soviet move and the American response in the form of the Reagan Doctrine, see Peter Rodman, *More Precious Than Peace* (New York, NY: Scribner's Sons, 1994), p. 217.
18. See, for example, "For Afghan Rebels, a Holy War 'to the Last Man,'" *The New York Times*, Dec. 19, 1984, pp. 12–13; or R. Watson, "Insurgencies: Two of a Kind," *Newsweek*, March 23, 1987, for positive coverage of Mujahidin whose "fundamentalist Islamic faith has made a holy war" and who managed to avoid defeat, despite "overwhelming odds."
19. In the Joint Commission's work, the extremely costly, albeit limited, standoff high in the Himalayas between the forces of India and Pakistan was discussed and preliminary steps nearly resolved.
20. For an account of the U.S. effort, see John Walcott, "The South Asia Two-Step," *Newsweek*, Nov. 4, 1985.

21. Gandhi was criticized in the domestic Indian press, which felt that India had acted like a supplicant before the United States in accepting the second-best computer technology.
22. As stated to the Indian Association of Foreign Affairs Correspondents, June 29, 1987.
23. Richard M. Weintraub, "Agreement Signed in Geneva: Pakistani Leader Predicts Turmoil," *The Washington Post*, April 15, 1988, p. A1.
24. For details of the negotiations, see Riaz M. Khan, *Untying the Afghan Knot: Negotiating Soviet Withdrawal* (Durham, NC: Duke University Press, 1992).
25. Michael R. Gordon, "U.S. and Moscow Agree on Pullout from Afghanistan," *The New York Times*, April 12, 1988, p. 1.
26. Remarks by President Reagan at the Heritage Foundation, Washington, DC, November 1987.
27. The first five-year $3.2 billion package covered the period from 1981 to 1986. The follow-on six-year agreement provided for $4.2 billion but was terminated in September 1990.
28. Speech by Robert C. McFarlane to the World Affairs Council of Washington, DC, Dec. 9, 1985.
29. Jagat Mehta, "Indian Policy and Afghanistan," *Indian Express*, March 29, 1989.
30. Stanley Heginbotham and Alyson Pyette, "Sri Lanka's Gamble for Ethnic Peace," Report for Congress, Congressional Research Service, July 29, 1987.
31. For example, "Subcontinental Detente?" Editorial, *The Wall Street Journal*, Oct. 22, 1985.
32. Chetan Kumar and Kanti Bajpai, "Operation Brass Tacks and Its Antecedents: A Nuclear and Security Chronology of South Asia, 1984–1987," unpublished manuscript, p. 13.
33. Ibid., p. 17.
34. Ibid.
35. In the midst of the crisis, Gandhi dismissed A. P. Venkateswaran as foreign secretary; contrary to most expectations, Venkateswaran had been conciliatory toward Pakistan.
36. For an account of the ways in which the Kashmir issue influences India-Pakistan relations, see Robert Wirsing, *India, Pakistan, and the Kashmir Dispute: On Regional Conflict and Its Resolution* (New York, NY: St. Martin's Press, 1994). For two versions of the events leading to the accession of Kashmir to India, see Alastair Lamb, *Kashmir: A Disputed Legacy, 1946–1990* (Karachi: Oxford University Press, 1992); and Prem Shankar Jha, *Kashmir, 1947: Rival Versions of History* (Delhi: Oxford University Press, 1996).
37. See, for example, annual reports of Amnesty International and Asia Watch.
38. Pakistan later attempted to win at least the propaganda war when Benazir Bhutto went to Sarajevo to show support for Bosnia, but it lost the policy fight at the Security Council when it showed neither leadership nor creative thinking despite the fact it had run for the Council seat as a large Muslim country.
39. "U.S. Defense Chief Urges Talk on Continent," *The New York Times*, Jan. 14, 1995, p. 4.
40. Comments to the Indian parliament, *The Hindustan Times*, April 28, 1989.
41. Statement by Assistant Secretary Richard Murphy before the Subcommittee on Asian and Pacific Affairs, House Foreign Affairs Committee, Feb. 25, 1987.

42. Yet women activists continued to support Benazir Bhutto and did not press for concessions. In any case, their numbers are limited, as the vast number of women in the electorate remain unrepresented.
43. Fasahat H. Syed, "U.S. Interests in South Asia—Past, Present and Future," *National Development and Security* 1, no. 4. (May 1993).
44. Membership of the consortium consists of Belgium, Canada, France, Germany, Italy, Japan, the Netherlands, Norway, Sweden, Switzerland, the United Kingdom, the United States, Asian Development Bank, European Commission, International Finance Corporation, IMF, Kuwait Fund for Arab Economic Development, Saudi Fund for Development, U.N. Resident Coordinator (UNDP/UNICEF/UNDCP/WHO), United Nations High Commission for Refugees, and the World Bank. Beyond the members, the following participate as observers: European Investment Bank, International Fund for Agricultural Development, Islamic Development Bank, Organization for Economic Cooperation and Development, and World Food Program.
45. P. M. Kamath, *The End of the Cold War: Implications for Indian-American Relations* (New Delhi: Indian Council of World Affairs, 1993), p. 65.
46. Talk of a review of the relationship with Israel by the Indian foreign office was circulating in early 1989.
47. John F. Burns, "U.S.-India Pact on Military Cooperation," statement by Perry at the signing, *The New York Times*, Jan. 13, 1995, p. 12.

CHAPTER 3

1. The Pressler amendment to Section 620 E of the Foreign Assistance Act of 1961 was enacted in 1985 with the following language: "(e) No assistance shall be furnished to Pakistan and no military equipment or technology be sold or transferred to Pakistan, pursuant to the authorities contained in this Act or any other Act, unless the President shall have certified in writing to the Speaker of the House of Representatives and the chairman of the Committee on Foreign Relations of the Senate, during the fiscal year in which the assistance is to be furnished or military equipment or technology is to be sold or transferred, that Pakistan does not possess a nuclear explosive device and that the proposed United States assistance program will reduce significantly the risk that Pakistan will possess a nuclear explosive device."
2. Only when the Nuclear Nonproliferation Act of 1978 precluded continued fuel supply without full-scope safeguards in India did the United States arrange for France to assume U.S. supply obligations.
3. For a discussion of the development of the Indian program, see James E. Katz and Onkar S. Marwah, *Nuclear Power in Developing Countries* (Lexington, MA: DC Heath and Company, 1981).
4. For details of the U.S.-Pakistan nuclear dispute, see Shirin Tahir-Kheli, *The United States and Pakistan: The Evolution of an Influence Relationship* (NY: Praeger, 1982).
5. Pierre Lellouche, "France in the International Nuclear Energy Controversy: A New Policy under Giscard d'Estaing," *Orbis* 22, no. 4 (1979), pp. 951–965.

6. The Symington amendment prohibits any form of assistance to any country that, after the passage of the International Security Assistance Act of 1971, delivers or receives nuclear enrichment equipment, materials, or technology. The Glenn amendment prohibits assistance if any country receives or delivers nuclear reprocessing equipment, materials, or technology.
7. For the view from the Department of State, see Dennis Kux, *India and the United States: Estranged Democracies, 1941–1991* (Thousand Oaks, CA: Sage Publications, 1994).
8. "Pakistanis Admit Gains in Uranium Technology," *The New York Times*, Feb. 25, 1985, p. 8.
9. *Indian Express*, Sept. 25, 1985.
10. Raja Ramanna, speaking to the IAEA in Vienna in the PTI report, *The Hindustan Times*, Sept. 25, 1985.
11. The later belief that Pakistani leaders could *not* be counted on to speak truthfully underlies much of the current distrust of Pakistan within the U.S. policy establishment, especially in Congress.
12. *The Hindu*, Oct. 25, 1985.
13. Elaine Sciolino, "U.N. Reviews about Gandhi Seem Mixed," *The New York Times*, Oct. 30, 1985, p. A9.
14. "An Interview with Rajiv Gandhi," *Time*, Oct. 21, 1985, p. 50.
15. Michael Getler and Don Oberdorfer, "Zia Says Soviet and Afghan Casualties Exceed 60,000," *The Washington Post*, Oct. 22, 1985, p. A1.
16. Gerald M. Boyd, "Reagan to See Indian and Pakistani Leaders," *The New York Times*, Oct. 22, 1985, p. 11.
17. *The Hindu*, Oct. 1, 1985; Stuart Auerbach, "India to Get High Tech U.S. Goods; Another Sign of Warmer Ties since Ghandi's Visit," *The Washington Post*, Oct. 15, 1985, p. D1.
18. Press conference, Oct. 27, 1985.
19. Joint press conference by President Reagan and Prime Minister Gandhi, the White House, Washington, DC, Oct. 20, 1987.
20. W. R. Doorner, "Knocking at the Nuclear Door," *Time*, March 30, 1987, pp. 42–43.
21. The White House, Office of the Press Secretary, Jan. 15, 1987.
22. Richard M. Weintraub, "Pakistan's Premier Points at Indian Fatal Bombing," *The Washington Post*, July 17, 1987, p. A22.
23. *The Sunday Observer* (London), March 1, 1987.
24. Speech by Undersecretary Armacost, "South Asia and the United States: An Evolving Partnership," The Asia Society, Washington, DC, April 29, 1987.
25. Analysis of American stated views by K. Subrahmanyam, "Pakistan's Nuclear Message," *Times of India*, March 7, 1987.
26. Statement by Deputy Assistant Secretary of Defense Edward W. Gnehm before the Subcommittee on Asian and Pacific Affairs, House Foreign Affairs Committee, May 14, 1987.
27. Ibid.
28. *The Sunday Observer*, London, March 1, 1987.
29. Statement by Senator John Glenn on assistance to Pakistan before the Senate Foreign Relations Committee, March 23, 1987, p. 7.

30. Ibid. Also, for a record of the U.S. legislature moves vis-à-vis the Pakistan nuclear program, see Leonard S. Spector, *The Undeclared Bomb* (Washington, DC: The Carnegie Endowment for International Peace, 1988), pp. 474–480.
31. Richard M. Weintraub and David Ottaway, "Afghan Rebels to Hit Foe Hard; U.S. Soviet Political Maneuvers Back Up Intensified Fighting," *The Washington Post*, July 6, 1987, p. A1.
32. Statement by Foreign Minister Yaqub Khan before a session of the parliament, Islamabad, April 20, 1987.
33. Address by Frank C. Carlucci, assistant to the president for national security affairs, to the India-U.S. Business Council, Washington, DC, May 13, 1987.
34. *The Hindu*, Dec. 7, 1987.
35. Comment by Dr. Raja Ramanna, in "Nuclear Scientist Criticizes U.S. Attitude," *Delhi Domestic Service in English*, Federal Broadcast Information Service (FBIS), Dec. 29, 1987, p. 48.
36. "Gandhi Welcomes U.S.-U.S.S.R. Missile Accord," *Delhi Domestic Service in English,* FBIS, Dec. 9, 1987, p. 51.
37. *Financial Express*, Sept. 10, 1987.
38. Interview of Prime Minister Gandhi with *Al-Jumhuriyah*, FBIS, Dec. 10, 1987, pp. 42–45.
39. Statement by Robert Peck, deputy assistant secretary of state for South Asia, before the Subcommittee on Asian and Pacific Affairs, House Foreign Affairs Committee, March 5, 1987.
40. *Times of India*, Dec. 28, 1987.
41. See George Perkovich, "A Nuclear Third Way in South Asia," *Foreign Policy*, no. 91 (Summer 1993), p. 86.
42. See Gates interview with Seymour Hersh, "On the Nuclear Edge," *The New Yorker*, March 29, 1993. Gates felt that Bhutto had given him the runaround and made herself unavailable.
43. Comments by Robert Oakley, *Conflict Prevention and Confidence-building in South Asia: The 1990 Crisis* (Washington, DC: The Henry L. Stimson Center, April 1994), pp. 8–9.
44. For the discussion of Indian policy, see P.R. Chari, *Indo-Pak Nuclear Standoff: The Role of the United States* (New Delhi: Manohar, 1995).
45. Statement by the Pakistan opposition leader, Nawaz Sharif, "South Asia's Nuclear Future," at the Carnegie Endowment Conference on Nuclear Nonproliferation and the Millennium, Washington, DC, Feb. 13, 1996, p. 6.
46. Statement by Arundhati Ghos, permanent representative of India to the Conference on Disarmament, Geneva, Jan. 25, 1996.
47. Speech at the Non-Aligned Movement summit, Cartagena, Colombia, Oct. 19, 1995.
48. Statement by Munir Akram, Pakistan's representative to the Conference on Disarmament, at the Carnegie Endowment for Peace Conference on Nuclear Non-Proliferation and the Millennium, Washington, DC, Feb. 13, 1996, p. 5.
49. Statement at the Conference on Disarmament, Geneva, Jan. 23, 1996.
50. Under the Pressler amendment, all assistance to Pakistan had been cut off in October 1990.

CHAPTER 4

1. For a discussion of American perceptions of Indian policies, See Dennis Kux, *India and the United States: Estranged Democracies*, 1941–1991 (Thousand Oaks, CA: Sage Publications, 1994).
2. Gobind Nankani of the World Bank, conversations with the author, Feb. 1994.
3. Ibid.
4. Interview with a leading industrialist in Bombay, March 1994.
5. The World Bank, *India Country Report* (Washington, DC: The World Bank, 1995.)
6. Shahid Javed Burki, "Is a South Asian Economic Miracle Possible?" address at the 15th Conference of the Association of Pakistan's Physicians in North America, Dallas, Aug. 13, 1994.
7. Statement by Robin Raphel, assistant secretary of state for South Asian Affairs, before the House Subcommittee on Asian and Pacific Affairs, Feb. 9, 1995.
8. Based on the unpublished paper "Is Economic Reform Possible under Democracy?," by Prem Shankar Jha, 1995.
9. Ibid., p. 16.
10. The World Bank, *India: Recent Economic Developments, and Prospects* (Washington, DC: The World Bank, 1995).
11. See, for example, Pete Engardi, "An Ultrasound Foothold in Asia," *Business Week*, Nov. 8, 1993, pp. 68–69.
12. John F. Burns, "India Economic Reforms Yield a Measure of Hope," *The New York Times*, Jan. 15, 1995, p. 10.
13. Ibid.
14. Special 301 is a 1988 amendment of the Trade and Tariff Act, which requires the U.S. trade representative to investigate countries that "have a history of violating existing laws and agreements dealing with intellectual property rights." Definition from I.M. Destler, *American Trade Politics* (Washington, DC: Institute for International Economics, 1995), p. 318.
15. The World Bank, "Pakistan Economic Update: Recent Developments and Medium-term Policy Agenda," (Washington, DC: The World Bank, 1994).
16. Ibid.
17. *Report of the Task Force on Energy,* Government of Pakistan, March 1994.
18. Toufiq A. Siddiqi, "India-Pakistan Cooperation on Energy and Environment," *Asian Survey* XXXV, no. 3 (1995), pp. 280–90.
19. Bhutto speech to energy-sector American investors, Washington, DC, April 6, 1995.
20. "Enron Offers an Accord on Its India Project," *The New York Times*, Sept. 20, 1995.
21. Rashid Ahmed, "Energy: On Again, Off Again," *Far Eastern Economic Review*, May 12, 1994, p. 62.

CHAPTER 5

1. See Seymour Hersh, "On the Nuclear Edge," *The New Yorker*, March 29, 1993.

2. See, for example, Samina Yasmeen and Aabha Dixit, *Confidence-building in South Asia* (Washington, DC: The Henry L. Stimson Center, 1995).
3. As he launched the Indian Action Plan, Rajiv Gandhi dwelt on the importance of any future arms control effort not only being fair but as being seen to be fair.
4. For example, Carnegie Endowment Study Group, *India and America after the Cold War* (Washington, DC: Carnegie Endowment for International Peace, 1993); and The Asia Society, *South Asia and the United States after the Cold War* (New York, NY: The Asia Society, 1994).
5. According to former U.S. Ambassador Robert B. Oakley in a 1996 statement.
6. For a discussion of negative and positive assurances and the possible role of the United Nations, see Stephen Hadley and Mitchell Reiss, *Nuclear Proliferation: Confronting the New Challenges* (New York, NY: Council on Foreign Relations, 1995), pp. 22–24.
7. Paula R. Newberg, *Double Betrayal: Repression and Insurgency in Kashmir* (Washington, DC: Carnegie Endowment for International Peace, 1995), p. 1.
8. The Clinton administration's lack of mention of Kashmir during the Indian prime minister's visit in 1994 spoke volumes about the difference between the administration's rhetoric on Kashmir and its policy. U.S. official pronouncements on the importance of human rights have little meaning if they are subscribed to only in the breach.

Index